The Letter in the Bottle

KAREN LIEBREICH has a doctorate in history from Cambridge University and a research diploma from the European University Institute in Florence. She has also worked as a cultural assistant for the French Institute in London and a documentary researcher and producer for television. Her previous book, *Fallen Order: Intrigue, Heresy and Scandal in the Rome of Galileo and Caravaggio*, was published by Atlantic Books in 2004.

'I love a good quest and could not speak to anyone until I'd finished *The Letter in the Bottle*. It's a lucid exposition of the simultaneous equation of love and pain that is being a mother, and moving but not remotely mawkish. Karen Liebreich has bottled this message perfectly.' Rachel Johnson, author of *The Mummy Diaries*

'Liebreich is forced to confront the motivations for her "Grail quest" and question her confidence in her intellectual powers. A book which is as haunting as it is elegant.' *Daily Telegraph*

The Letter in the Bottle

A TRUE STORY

Karen Liebreich

ATLANTIC BOOKS
LONDON

First published in Great Britain in 2006 by Atlantic Books,
an imprint of Grove Atlantic Ltd.

This revised paperback edition published in Great Britain
in 2010 by Atlantic Books.

1 3 5 7 9 8 6 4 2

A CIP catalogue record for this book
is available from the British Library.

ISBN: 978 1 84887 577 7

Printed in Great Britain by CPI Bookmarque

Atlantic Books
An imprint of Grove Atlantic Ltd
Ormond House
26–27 Boswell Street
London WC1N 3JZ

www.atlantic-books.co.uk

Contents

On Sunday 17 February 2002 a bottle
containing a letter washed up on the beach
at Warden Bay, Isle of Sheppey, Kent.

After a seven year search, the author
of the letter finally made contact . . .

'Un livre est une bouteille jetée en pleine mer sur laquelle il faut coller cette etiquette: attrape qui peut.'

'A book is a bottle cast into the open sea on which the label reads: catch me if you can.'

Alfred de Vigny, *Journal d'un poète*, 1797–1863

'Writing a book is like throwing a message in a bottle into the sea. You can't control who reads your book.'

Philip Pullman, BBC Radio 4, 17 November 2003

1

The bottle lay washed up on the mud at the high-tide mark. Very blue, bright, shaped like a teardrop, it was untouched by the debris and seaweed that surrounded it.

She had taken a break from work to walk the dogs. Suddenly overwhelmed by the backlog facing her, she had turned away from her desk, summoned her dogs, and headed out to the car.

Warden Bay was not the nearest beach. It was a twenty-minute drive, but its bleakness suited her mood. She crossed from the mainland to the Isle of Sheppey, enjoying the flat, open landscape after the claustrophobia of work. In winter at low tide the grey mud of Warden Bay stretched away into the distance. The lack of features and sheer sameness attracted none of the visitors who frequented Beachy Head, with its dramatic shores, helpful car parks, convenient road access and plunging cliffs. No one visited Warden Bay in winter, although tough children who lived on the wind-blown estate behind the muddy hillocks sometimes threw supermarket trolleys down on to the shore below.

She had been on the beach for about twenty minutes, muffled against the cold and damp by an ancient black leather jacket zipped up to the chin and a bobble hat pulled low over her forehead. The dogs bounded around happily, a few hundred metres from her, keeping an eye on the general direction of travel. Their coats, rendered drab brown and black by the grey winter light, blended into the pebbles of the beach and on the rare occasions when they stood still to sniff something particularly interesting, they were almost perfectly camouflaged. Only their movement made them visible.

The blue of the bottle was a sudden splinter of colour which she saw from a distance as she made her way along the beach, shoulders hunched against the oncoming wind. Its glow belonged to a different clime, where the sun shone and the sea was a proper blue. It lay at the tide mark, where the grey mud met the grey pebbles.

She drew close, bent and picked up the bottle, drawn by its irresistible colour and its fragile smoothness. She felt she could no more have left it there ungathered than she could have abandoned her own child on the beach. Maybe she would use it as a vase for single flowers in some far-off spring. A voice told her she already had a shelf-full of dusty scavenged bottles in her kitchen, but this one was different. The shape was unusual; an Evian teardrop of blue, it would have stood out even in a bright supermarket full of garish primary colours. On the monochrome beach the effect was startling. As she crouched over it, lying slick and gleaming in the woolly palm of her glove, she saw that there was a slim scroll of paper within.

Something stirred within her. A message in a bottle. A fragment of excitement on a dreary day, in a dreary month, after what had turned out to be a dreary year. She tried to unscrew the top but her gloved hands slipped on the glass, and a light drizzle had misted the bottle's surface. Rather than risk ruining the message, she contained her excitement, whistled to her companions and turned for home. The dogs, caught unawares by the change of direction, raced to catch her up.

Back home, as she dried the dogs' paws, and made herself a cup of tea, her thoughts fixed on the bottle containing the scroll. Was it a love letter? A plea for rescue? Or only kids messing around? She knew it would be special because the tide had not smashed it, the mud had not buried it, and the local children had not found it first and broken it. It was as if it had been sent to her.

She took her mug and the bottle through to the living room and settled down on the sofa. In the corners the dogs were licking the grit and salt from between their paws. A smell of wet dog filled the room.

The bottle seemed to glow with promise, and she felt reluctant to break the delicious thrill of anticipation. Finally she put down her mug, picked up the bottle, and tried to twist the cap. It was a strange pointed shape, and offered her little grip. She struggled for some time, then, suddenly, it yielded.

The seal had been secured by a strip of white tape, and the letter was dry. She upended the bottle over the coffee table and the roll slid out, tied by a pale blue ribbon, along with a sprinkle of perfumed wood shavings. Very gently she undid the narrow ribbon, and uncurled the papers. A lock of curled hair fell from the pages. Between her fingers she held two sheets, densely written in blue ink, which were struggling to re-roll themselves. The writing was looped and foreign, and her schoolgirl French was barely sufficient to decipher the first words.

She felt a pang of disappointment. It seemed she would have to wait to find out what the message contained, though it seemed appropriate that the bottle should hold on to its secret for a little longer. As she held the letter to her nose and inhaled the sweet smell from the sandalwood shavings that had cradled the scroll, she thought about whom she could ask to translate the letter. The bottle was so carefully chosen, the ribbon, the lock of hair, the scented shavings so carefully assembled and prepared with such tenderness that the contents would surely not disappoint.

4

She left the bottle and its contents lying scattered over her table and went over to the telephone.

2

Although I had agreed immediately to look at the letter, I was still annoyed when it arrived a day or two later. I was trying desperately to meet an important deadline, and had no time to spare. I had listened with half an ear to the description of how the letter had been found, and the prompt arrival of a few pages of intricately written French came at a bad moment. My friend had not replaced the letter in the bottle, but had simply posted the pages on to me, roughly flattened, in a recycled envelope without any accompanying note. When I unfolded the sheets and saw the looped handwriting with the *r*'s and the *n*'s that could be read as *u*'s, my spirits sank. I skimmed the first few lines half-heartedly. This would take some effort to decipher, and I put it aside to deal with when I had more time.

A few weeks later I took the letter from my in-tray and started to translate, typing directly as I read, without letting the meaning run ahead of my fingers.

To all ships at sea, to all ports of call, to my family, to all friends and strangers.

This is a message, a prayer. The message is that my sufferings have taught me a great truth.

I already had (a long time ago) what everyone is searching for, and few ever find, the only person in the world whom I was born to love for ever, my first son, Maurice. A child rich in simple treasures, that no wind . . . no storm . . . not even death could ever destroy. The prayer is for all mothers to know such a love and be healed by it. If my prayer is answered, it will erase all errors . . . all regrets . . . and soothe all anger.

Please, God . . .

My life started when he was born, and I thought it was over when he left me one summer's evening, never to return. He was thirteen years old . . . Without warning, he slipped away from life in an excess of desires, too full of vivid life, at the dawn of summer. For a long time he travelled between two waters, between two lights, trying tirelessly to use up the

7

strength in his outstretched arms. He submitted to the silence, the terrors and the cold, but he discovered the secret ways of the universe, the infinite movement of our origins, and the wanderings of the stars.

He didn't know that I, his mother, fed him with my thoughts to grant him eternal life in memory, to keep him whole within my flesh.

Forgive me, my son, my love . . . I thought that by clinging to your memory in this way I would keep us both alive for as long as possible. Forgive me, my son, for not having spoken to you for such a long time. I felt I was lost, without my bearings. I kept crashing into things, stumbling everywhere . . . I had never been lost before you left me. You showed me the north, I always found my way, for you were my way.

Forgive me for being so angry at your disappearance. I still think there's been some mistake, and I keep waiting for God to fix it.

I'm doing better now, my love. The road has been long, very long, but through it all you have supported me.

A few nights ago, you appeared to me in a dream, and your smile rocked me like a child. I understood that it was time for me to let you go.

You stayed close to me for all these years . . . I clung on with all my despair to what was no longer and what would never be again.

My infinity, I thought this suffering bound me to you. It consumed me until it left no room for anything else, but I began to permit it to leave my heart, my soul, my very being. Thanks to you, my love, I succeeded in transforming this suffering into love, into life. All that I remember of this dream is a feeling of peace, for you, for me. When I awoke I still felt it, and I tried to keep the feeling alive for as long as possible.

I am writing to you, Maurice, to tell you that I am embarking on the search for this peace, and to beg your forgiveness for so many things. Forgive me for not having known how to protect you from death. Forgive me for not having been able to find the words at that terrible moment when you slid through my fingers, to express what I felt, and above all for not having held you so tightly that God would not have been able to take you away.

There is no moment in my life, my son, where you are not present. How many paths travelled before I was able to listen and hear the sound of my pain, of our pain.

Your thirteen years of life brought me infinite happiness.

Today, I know that you were just passing through to show me the way, to reveal how I could lead my life, and by leaving

9

me you invited me to dare to change something that I could not envisage until then. You had the power to say, through your presence, however fleeting, and your brutal disappearance, 'Mum, dare [to live] your life, only you will live it.' Today I am listening and I hear the message that my son has sent me, my son whose ephemeral life has wounded me for ever because I was deaf to his message for so long.

Today the journey is ending, my son has reached harbour again, on a faraway shore, close to the rising sun. He has once more found the light vessel of his childhood that will lead him gently towards the peace he has attained.

So my dear, my love, I let the balloon rise to the skies, serenely, with all the tenderness of a mother.

May this bottle thrown far from the shore stay forever rocked by the ocean, in the ebb and flow of the rolling waves.

While God gives me life, I promise you to live it to the full, to savour each instant in richness and in serenity.

I know that we will find one another again, when the time comes. God owes it to us.

Farewell my son, farewell my love.

I love you with all my heart, with all my soul, and I am proud to have been your mother. Fly away in peace.

Go, my love, go towards the light, my gentle seagull. May

the source of your soul surge and run murmuring towards the sea, and unfold like the innumerable petals of a lotus flower.

It may be that most of us write our own life story, making it up as we go through life, but there are those whose lives seem written in advance, inescapable, and which form a perfect circle. There are others whose course is unforeseeable, sometimes incomprehensible. What I have had the sorrow of losing in my life has taught me what is most precious, just as it has taught me about this love for which I can only be grateful.

This letter, my son, I intend to share with only one person, the only friend I will keep all my life, and beyond. She is called Christine, she is gentleness itself.

I had no preconceptions when I started deciphering and translating the letter. It was long, and I figured it would probably take me an hour just to type out the rough translation. But as I began to read I was almost immediately swept along by the emotional journey of the unknown mother who had lost her son. How does one come to terms with that? How can one continue living? How had he died? As I translated and typed I began to fear that the letter was a suicide note. In the middle, I broke off and turned to the end, dreading a final farewell as the mother jumped off the cliff to join her son. But the last few lines made no sense without the rest of the letter, so I had to go back to where I had stopped. I typed faster, making the translation as literal as possible, rushing to discover what had happened. As I translated, I wept, and my partner, working quietly behind me, looked round curiously. I could not stop to recover my composure until I knew how the letter would end. But as the mother promised her son that she would 'live [life] to the full' and 'savour each instant in richness and in serenity' my anxiety eased. By the end of the letter I felt emotionally wrung out by the horror of the writer's experience and the rawness of her grief. Who was she? What had happened to Maurice? Where was she now?

I kept the letter but sent the translation to my friend, and turned back to my own work with relief.

3

I heard nothing for several days. Finally I asked my friend whether she had received the translation and what she thought.

'It's awful,' she said almost in a whisper, and I could hear her voice breaking. She too had been devastated by the letter. A single mother, with a thirteen-year-old son herself, she found the message almost unbearable, and it took her several attempts to read to the end. When she had picked up the bottle on the beach that day, she had thought of romance, mystery, the glamour of a message from a distant shore. But it was far from the casual love letter she had imagined. She later told me that for days after discovering the contents she had been depressed and emotional, mourning Maurice's death in sympathy with the unknown mother. She grew quietly more protective of her own son. She offered to take him to his football matches; she walked the first few streets with him when he set off for school in the mornings; she dropped him off when he went to meet his friends, so that he wouldn't have to catch the bus alone.

The death of a child is unimaginable. The mind shies away from it, but when I held this letter in my hand I was forced to confront it. Although my friend had found the bottle, I felt the letter it contained was written to me. And it was addressed to me, the stranger, 'l'inconnu'. Apart from the unknown friend, Christine, I was the first person to hold the paper the unknown mother had written on, and I had been the first to read and understand her message of desperation.

It was a personal letter. It started off addressing all strangers, but narrowed its focus into a private message to her son. But the final paragraphs seemed to open up a more universal message, a message that 'life has taught me what is most precious' which echoed the opening lines, that 'all mothers [should] know such a love and be healed by it'. There was an ambivalence in the letter about keeping her grief secret and sharing it with the world, an ambivalence reflected in the secrecy of writing a private letter and then throwing it out to sea, addressed to all strangers in any port of call anywhere in the world.

Somehow discussing the terrible contents of the letter with my friend seemed to make it more real, and that night I could not sleep, trying to turn my mind away from the grief of the unknown mother. I tried not to dwell on how many sleepless nights she must have suffered. How she must have felt that the very marrow of her soul had turned black. It was the grinding, inescapable misery of her loss that kept me company that night.

Usually I avoid thinking about such an all-consuming loss. Why should I torture myself with imagining my own child dead? Whenever a child goes missing and a school photograph of its bright little face shines out from the front page of the newspaper or the television screen, sympathy for the family is mixed with horror that such crimes could exist. But above all there is the fear that it could be our child. No one can fail to be moved by such stories, but only for a parent would the loss of a child resonate with quite such emotional impact. With stories in the news, you can distance yourself from the victims. The very fact that the death is reported in the media makes it seem more remote and so more bearable. But this letter was a direct cry of such anguish.

The letter had dropped through my front door unadorned by the mystique of its beautiful bottle and without any warning of tragedy or mystery, and its contents had hit me unawares with the full force of their stark message. Sitting comfortably before my keyboard, fresh from the banality of the school run and the everyday administration of family life, I had been dropped into another human being's tragedy – a death which had transformed this unknown person's life, and whose words, cast on to the sea, had somehow washed up on my desk.

In the days that followed I too became more protective of my children. I saw them through new eyes and held them closer as they set off for school. I was overwhelmed with sadness for the unknown mother. I grieved that she had no flesh of her flesh for whom she could smooth down an errant lock of hair, or to whom she could give a careless hug. Any parent is familiar with the fear of failing to protect one's child, of failing to shepherd him or her to maturity. Anyone who has loved knows the fear of loss. At some level the letter represented a universal message; it symbolized the anxiety all mothers feel about their children. And yet it was a very individual tale of tragedy.

I mourned with the writer, but I was also intrigued. Who was she? How did the boy die? What really happened? And I wanted desperately to know that she was now doing better, that the words of reassurance she had written were true, that she had found a way to live with her grief and even to enjoy her life once more.

I was just plain curious. Curious to know who she was, what she was like, curious to know what had happened to her son. I had always thought of drivers who slow down to look at roadside crashes as intrusive rubber-neckers, but perhaps that element of curiosity has a more complex motivation: if I know how that crash occurred, I could avoid the same thing happening to me. And of course I am thankful that the accident has not happened to me. And somehow this letter from an unknown mother – a mother whose whole life had been absorbed in her son's, and who had lost him in some appalling way – represented something of this car-crash mentality. The uneasy blend of curiosity and sympathy seemed to react together and produced not only a cautionary tale but a captivating mystery.

A few days later I called my friend the dog-walker for a chat, and the conversation soon turned to the letter in the bottle. While she too wanted to know more, I sensed that for her it would just remain one of life's mysteries and that she was trying to put the bleak message out of her mind and get on with her life. For me it was different. The letter continued to haunt my thoughts over the next few weeks, and gradually the desire grew in me to find out more. Could the mother be found?

I was plagued by unworthy emotions: I wanted to know how Maurice had died; I wanted to know what his mother was like; I wanted to know whether I could track the origin of an unsigned letter in a bottle. I wanted the writer to know that the bottle had been found intact and beautiful on an English shore and that I had read her letter. I wanted to reassure myself that she was all right, that the optimistic impulse at the end of the letter had lasted. I wanted to know that there was life after death; that it was possible to recover from such an event, if not unscathed, then at least able to continue a meaningful existence.

And if, by some amazing piece of detective work or good fortune,

I did find her, how would I approach her? As a mother? But didn't I run the risk of seeming to gloat about my living children, while she mourned her dead son? Would I turn up on her doorstep, bottle in hand, smiling brightly? Would she be at all curious about who had found her letter or annoyed that I had interrupted its journey? Would she be pleased that people who cared had found it? Had she really meant it to 'stay forever rocked by the ocean', or had she wanted 'all strangers' to find it and share her emotions, as she also said in her letter?

There were no answers to these questions. If I discovered her identity and whereabouts, I could plan how – or even whether – to approach her. If she came forward in response to some appeal or advertisement, then she would have made her own decision about whether to be found. Either way, it was easy to postpone thinking about any actual meeting with her. It seemed so far away and so unlikely.

The real facts in the letter were sparse.

1. The son was called Maurice.
2. He was thirteen years old when he died.
3. He was her first son.
4. He died one evening, 'at the dawn of summer'.

5. The letter-writer, the mother, had a close friend called Christine.

6. There was some material evidence, such as the bottle itself, the paper, the ribbon, the ink, the wood shavings, the lock of hair.

There were some other clues. Were they concrete signs, or simply metaphors?

1. 'He slipped away from life in an excess of desires'.

2. 'For a long time he travelled between two waters, between two lights.'

3. She begged forgiveness for not having spoken to him 'for such a long time'. Either he died a while ago, or they had not spoken for some time before his death.

4. 'That terrible moment when you slid through my fingers.'

5. 'My son has reached harbour again, on a faraway shore, close to the rising sun.'

At first I took these clues literally.

The letter-writer was clearly fairly well educated. She had read some Buddhist works, and imbibed some New Age vocabulary. She spoke of God but there were no biblical references, no references to Jesus. Sometimes she referred to 'Dieu' with a capital letter, sometimes in lower case. Was this a significant variation or just sloppiness? Did it imply a Protestant who addresses God directly, or a Catholic who remains at a respectful distance? Either way, she was annoyed with him – he had made a serious error by taking her son away, he owed her a recompense. There was no mention of a man, a partner or a father. There was no mention of any other children, though the fact that Maurice was her 'first son' implied that he had siblings. There was no mention of Maurice's childhood, other than the comment that her life had begun with his birth. This expression in itself implied a level of intensity in the relationship between mother and son that neither I nor my friend could completely identify with: I felt I had had an enjoyable and worthwhile life before having children; this woman did not. Or perhaps the death of her son had so altered her perception of her previous life that, in hindsight, only his existence had validated hers. Life after the death of a child can never be the same, but does it cancel out all that went before?

Maurice's birth had somehow transformed his mother from a non-person into something real. She seemed to be utterly fused with him – I remembered that feeling from the earliest days of mother-hood, when independent existence had only just begun for my child and I was still coming to terms with his emergence. But then one tries to build independence for one's children, and encourage them gently to stand and walk on through life. I remember being shocked by a friend who was still breastfeeding when her child was five, and think-ing it reflected her need of him, not any nutritional requirement on his part. Surely by the age of thirteen, such a fusion is no longer a healthy bond.

There was a great deal of watery imagery in the letter, many refer-ences to waves and floating – and some mention of light and air. There was no mention of the earth: no suggestion of returning to dust, no fruits of the loins, none of the traditional allusions to death and decay. There were no childhood anecdotes, no sentimental refer-ences to any of the signposts of growth other than his birth. By the end of the letter Maurice was in splendour, while his mother remained in the water. The letter represented a kind of voyage through her most intimate emotions, from the water to the sky, to a crescendo of grief and a kind of serenity.

But none of this provided much concrete information.

Were there any clues in the name itself? After all, the name made up half the certain facts about the boy: that he was called Maurice and was aged thirteen. Was there a region in France that produced most of the Maurices? It seemed unlikely.

In the catalogue of saints, Maurice was a Roman soldier, martyred around AD 287 in modern-day Switzerland, patron saint of infantry-men, dyers and weavers. He was particularly called upon by those suffering from cramps. His feast-day was 22 September. According to various name dictionaries, Maurice had no particular regional links.

It is an old-fashioned name. An uncommon name. A name from the turn of the century – even from the last century. A name linked to that archetypical Frenchman, Maurice Chevalier, who thanked Heaven for little girls.

Perhaps not a name for the child of a Parisian intellectual. More likely to be a name for a worker at a Renault factory. A name for a fisherman. Or, in this case, a name for a dead child.

After translating the letter I had sent it back to my friend. She had refolded it exactly as it had been, and with great difficulty reinserted it into the narrow neck of the bottle and placed it on a kitchen shelf, with her other beach flotsam, where she occasionally glanced at it while doing the washing-up. Although our friendship was close, we seldom met, since she rarely visited London, and the only time I had gone to her house in Kent had been for her wedding many years before. We talked on the phone often, but we only met once every two or three years, and always in London. But I was obsessed with the letter she had found, and wanted to know more. I wanted to know what the bottle looked like – in her somewhat inarticulate way she had said it was different and beautiful. How could a bottle be beautiful? Or different, for that matter? In retrospect I now realize that my willingness to undertake the three-hour drive from the wrong side of London to one of Kent's less accessible corners should have warned me that I was becoming sucked into something. But, at the time, I made excuses about not having seen her for a while and suggested I come down for lunch. I asked whether I could see the bottle, and whether she could show me the beach where she had found it.

I drove down to Kent and when my friend brought the bottle from the kitchen, I realized why she had spoken of it with such enthusiasm. It was a very striking and beautiful teardrop shape, a very bright colour, a special bottle.

We took our dogs and walked together on the beach and I wondered that she should choose such an unattractive location. I thought Warden Bay was one of the ugliest beaches I had ever visited. The texture of the mud was glutinous; the distance of the sea at low tide made the water a remote and uninspiring presence; the location of the beach between council and industrial estates was uninviting. My friend admitted she only came here when she was feeling really low and then it struck a chord of sympathy with her.

Back at her house, I asked if I could borrow the bottle with its letter. She agreed readily, but as she handed it over to me, her eyes gleamed momentarily, like Bilbo's when he is forced to pass over the ring to the next bearer. The mystery and beauty of the bottle, allied to its tragic message, created a possessiveness that I would grow to understand in the weeks and months that passed. Once she relinquished it she seemed almost relieved. Amid reassurances that I would return the bottle once I had had a good look at it, and would guard it against all harm, I left with my own filthy, beach-beslimed dog shortly afterwards.

That night I lifted the bottle out of the protective cardboard box I had placed it in, unwrapped the tissue paper, and set it on the kitchen table. My partner took his newspaper and retired to another room. I stared at the bottle, enjoying its shape and colour, and wondering once more about the woman who had sent it. I was beginning to realize that the search for her would not be easy. In the past I had tracked documents through the labyrinthine archives of Europe's oldest libraries, I had hunted down secretive old Nazis who had eluded the authorities for years, I had delved into the cupboards of the Vatican's restricted archives, but maybe this quest would defeat me. As the warm kitchen light was reflected back from the dense blue glass, the bottle seemed to be issuing a challenge. Go on, it appeared to be saying. Use those linguistic and detective skills of which you are so proud, find out about me . . .

I wrapped the bottle carefully, extinguishing its teasing glow with a vindictive flick of tissue paper, and buried it in its cardboard box. I would take up the challenge.

4

'Lancer, jeter une bouteille à la mer: lancer un message en espérant qu'il trouvera un destinataire.'

'To throw a bottle into the sea: "to throw out a message in the hope that it will find its destination."'

Le Petit Larousse, 1998

I cannot remember the first time I became aware that bottles could contain messages. It is a fact of life that I always knew, a part of my consciousness from childhood adventure stories. As far back as I can remember I always knew that letters could be sent in bottles, though I had never sent one myself, or found one. Friends and acquaintances recalled sending them as children, and one or two had even found letters in bottles, simple little requests for penfriends from other children on holiday by the seaside.

There is an irresistible charm associated with a letter in a bottle; the frivolous way it travels, driven by the currents, the wind and pure chance; the incongruity of its appearance, a tiny solid element in its vast watery setting. Its transparency immediately reveals that there is something inside, written by one person to whoever may be out there. The hopeful optimism, against all the odds, that a soul mate might find it washed up somewhere on a distant shore. And, in this case, the desperation that must have driven the mother to write her letter and fling it out into the sea. A mother reduced to casting forth letters to her dead son. Letters from one unknown person to another.

The concept of a letter in a bottle certainly implies that such a letter is written in the hope that someone will find it. In the library I found an article on how to create the perfect letter in a bottle. Ed Sobey, an oceanographer and sea-ice specialist, has researched the subject and analysed the best methods of ensuring the bottle floated at the correct angle and level in the water:

> Take a small soda bottle. The type with the screw-on lid is best. The first step is to ballast the bottle. Put some dry sand in the bottle, and place it in a bucket of water. Find the amount of sand necessary to weight the bottle without sinking it. The bottle should float, neck down, with only ½in. of freeboard when in the ocean. Fresh water and salt water have different densities, so if the bottle floats correctly in fresh

water, more sand will be needed to make it float properly in sea water . . . Screw on the original lid or place a rubber stopper or bottle top on the bottle. As an added measure, dip the cap and bottle neck in liquid paraffin.

Through the years people have turned to bottles to test ocean currents, to transmit news, to spread the Gospel, to advertise their products, to send messages of love and hope, and to launch pleas for rescue. Over a period of nearly twenty years Dutch beachcomber Wim Kruiswijk analysed 435 bottles that washed up on to Holland's coasts. Seventy-five per cent of these contained requests for pen pals or simply a return address. Of the remainder:

36 contained jokes

27 – religious pamphlets

12 – love letters

10 – 'messages related to sociological studies'

9 – drawings

4 – pornographic letters

3 – requests for help

2 – advertisements

1 – a letter protesting about pollution

Would Kruiswijk have classified the letter to Maurice as a love letter, a request for help, or a matter 'related to sociological studies'?

The earliest recorded letter in a bottle was around 310 BC when the Greek philosopher Theophrastus threw sealed bottles into the Mediterranean in an effort to prove that the inland sea was linked to the Atlantic. There was no recorded response.

In the 1490s, Christopher Columbus noted in his log that on the trip back to Spain after the discovery of the New World he was caught in a terrible storm. Afraid that the important news of his discovery might be lost, he wrote a short report, accompanied with a note requesting the finder to send it on to the Spanish Queen, sealed it into a cask and had it thrown overboard. It was lucky that the storm abated, and Columbus survived, because his message did not arrive.

It is widely reported that in the 1580s Queen Elizabeth I appointed an official Uncorker of Ocean Bottles and made it a crime for anyone else to open such bottles, which occasionally may have contained messages about enemy positions, or secret communications from spies. However, although the story has a certain romance, it seems likely to be a myth.

In 1714 – or some say 1784 – Chunosuke Matsuyama was shipwrecked with his crew of forty-four off a small island, while treasure-hunting in the Pacific. His plea for rescue arrived centuries

29

too late, in 1935. Legend has it that the bottle was washed up on the very beach where Matsuyama grew up.

Meanwhile, beachcombing was becoming an acceptable leisure pursuit. By the mid-eighteenth century scholars and ladies of leisure, clutching notebooks and sketchpads and seeking interesting driftwood and items of natural historical interest, were a common sight on the beaches of Europe. One historian described beachcombing in England in the 1760s as 'a full-fledged mania among people from all walks of life'.

In May 1859, Dr Livingstone left a message in a bottle at the mouth of the Zambezi River on the Indian Ocean in what is today Mozambique. He had just returned to the coast from his second expedition to the African interior, hoping to pick up some salt and other provisions before setting off once more. After waiting a week in vain for the errant paddle steamer containing his supplies, Livingstone addressed his letter to an unnamed 'Commander of Her Majesty's Ship', the ship's name also being left blank. He explained that the expedition would be leaving the following morning and that he would be placing the bottle 'ten feet Magnetic North from a mark (+) cut on the beacon on the island off this harbour': superfluous information, one would have thought, since anyone reading the letter would already have found the bottle. The beacon had been erected by the navy the previous year, and Livingstone had agreed with Admiral

Kongone Harbour
25 May 1859

To ____

Commander of Her Majesty's
Ship ____

Sir

We have been at the
Luabo - Melambe and Kongone
mouths of the Zambesi since the 18th
in hopes of meeting one of H. M.'s

Grey that any passing man-o'-war would check its base for reports and letters. By the time the letter was found by HMS *Persian*, Livingstone and his companions were back in the interior on their way to discovering Lake Nyasa, the future Lake Malawi. The letter resurfaced in 1905 among the papers of Admiral Sir James Donnet, who may have been on the ship that retrieved the bottle. Eventually it was bought at Sotheby's by the explorer Quentin Keynes, who was a serial collector.

In the 1950s Keynes had become fascinated by the quagga, a kind of semi-striped zebra presumed to be extinct. His worldwide searches failed to discover any remaining beasts, so he turned his attention to the giant sable antelope, and thence to the spotted zebra. By 1958 Keynes was so obsessed with the history of Dr Livingstone, and this bottle, that he made a special trip to the Zambezi, only to find that the island where the bottle had been buried had been washed away. However, the grandson of a guide of Livingstone's directed him towards a nearby baobab tree, seventy-two feet in circumference, on which he was thrilled to discover that Livingstone had carved his initials. On Keynes's death, his possessions, which included material on James Joyce, St Helena, elephants, the explorer Sir Richard Burton and the Galapagos islands – as well as the quagga and the dodo – were put up for auction. The letter, Lot 431, fetched £15,000.

In 1902, the polar explorer Evelyn Baldwin wrote in Norwegian and English: 'Five ponies and 150 dogs remain. Desire hay, fish and 30 sledges. Must return early in August. Baldwin.' The bottle containing his message was not picked up until 1948, by a Russian fisherman, but by then Baldwin was long – and safely – returned.

On 9 September 1914, Private Thomas Hughes, aged twenty-six, of Stockton-on-Tees wrote to his wife, Elizabeth, as he left for the battlefields of France.

Dear Wife,

I am writing this note on this boat and dropping it into the sea just to see if it will reach you.

If it does, sign this envelope on the right hand bottom corner where it says receipt. Put the date and hour of receipt and your name where it says signature and look after it well.

Ta ta sweet, for the present. Your Hubby.

He added a covering note asking the finder to forward the letter, slid it into a green ginger-beer bottle with a screw-on rubber top, and threw it into the English Channel. Two days later the Second Durham Light Infantry came under fire and Hughes was killed. His matter-of-fact little message drifted for eighty-five years until it was found by a Thames fisherman, Steve Gowan. Intrigued by the story, Gowan discovered that although Elizabeth had died twenty years earlier in New Zealand, the Hugheses' daughter, who had been only two when the letter was written, was still alive and able to receive the message from her dead father hand-delivered by the fisherman.

In May 1915, as the torpedoed Cunard liner *Lusitania* sank, a passenger wrote the following message in a bottle: 'I am still on deck with a few people. One is a child. The last boats have left. We are sinking fast. The orchestra is still playing bravely. The end is near. Maybe this note . . .' Here the message broke off abruptly. Maybe this note will be found by rescuers in time? Maybe this note will preserve our memory?

Probably the first occasion when an evangelist took seriously the message in Ecclesiastes – 'Cast thy bread upon the waters, for thou shalt find it after many days' (11:1) – occurred in April 1940. George Phillips of Puget Sound, Washington, was on the beach one day 'and I saw the tide carrying driftwood. Why couldn't I spread the gospel in the same way?' As an alcoholic, Phillips was of course familiar with sources of used spirits bottles and he gave up his work in real estate and the used-car business to concentrate full time on his preaching-by-bottle efforts. In a pleasing irony the objects that once contained what he now perceived as the vice of alcohol were used to carry the Word of the Lord. He sent off some 40,000 bottles, and received 1,500 answers. His messages, dubbed Gospel Bombs, travelled as far afield as the Pacific Coast, Australia, Mexico, Hawaii and New Guinea.

In 1943, Maja Westerman fled Nazi-occupied Estonia and took refuge on the island of Gotska Sandoen, an island so isolated that it still has no proper wharf and visitors must leap from the boat to shore. Cut off from news, Maja sent a message in a bottle requesting information about the war:

Dear friend, we live on an island. We came here a year ago
. . . the lighthouse keeper's family is very kind . . . Is the war
finished? . . . We wait for peace and friendship.

It was not until 2003 that a Swiss tourist visiting a beach on the
Swedish mainland discovered it.

In 1948, Dean Bumpus of the Woods Hole Oceanographic
Institution in Massachusetts spotted the scientific possibilities of
bottle travel by pioneering a major study of coastal circulation off
the Eastern United States, throwing as many as 20,000 bottles into
the Atlantic.

In 1954 A. W. Fawcett, managing director of Guinness Exports
Ltd, based in Liverpool, devised the first of two advertising 'bottle-
drops' in which 50,000 specially sealed Guinness® beer bottles, empty
except for certificates and booklets, were dropped from merchant
ships at eleven different locations in the Atlantic, Pacific and Indian
Oceans. Buoyed up by the success of this venture, and to celebrate the
two-hundreth anniversary of the first Arthur Guinness brewery in
Dublin, a few years later Mr Fawcett organized the dropping of some
150,000 specially embossed bottles into the Atlantic Ocean from
thirty-eight different ships over a period of six weeks, starting on 14
July 1959. Each bottle contained a small number of documents,
including a certificate 'from the office of King Neptune'. There was

also a little booklet telling the story of the Guinness brand, a special gold-coloured 1759–1959 label, and some instructions on how to turn the bottle into a table-lamp for those so inclined. Some of the bottles contained other items such as an advertisement for Ovaltine (which helped to sponsor the bottle-drop) or a notice about the ship that dropped it. The press office concludes happily, 'As bottles from both bottle-drops are still turning up today we can definitely say that these are our longest-running advertising promotions!'

In 1956, Martin Douglas went out in his powered yacht off the Florida coast and was never seen again. Two years later a jamjar washed up on Avoca Beach, north of Sydney, Australia. Inside was a hastily penned will, written on successive blank cheques torn out of Douglas's chequebook, along with an unemotional summary of his increasingly desperate situation:

> Should this note be found, please forward it to my wife, Alice Douglas, at Miami Beach, Florida. No doubt you're wondering what became of me. I got blown out into the water due to engine trouble.

In 1979, the pop group Police released their hit single 'Message in a Bottle'. They send 'an SOS to the world', and for a year no one answers. Then, suddenly, 'a hundred billion bottles' arrive on the beach; the lonely cry for help, linked to the catchy tune, evoked a powerful response in the millions who bought the record.

In 2002 a solitary woman walking her dogs on a beach in Kent discovered a blue Evian bottle with a message from another lonely woman.

5

Before throwing myself wholeheartedly into the search for the unknown author, I thought I would start by looking at the statistics. Exactly how big was this haystack in which I thought to search for my needle? Given that Maurice travelled 'for a long time . . . between two waters, between two lights' and 'reached harbour again, on a faraway shore, close to the rising sun', I was clearly looking for a boy who had died by drowning, perhaps in a stretch of water such as the English Channel with lighthouses at each coast. A harbour on the eastern shore narrowed down the location still further.

I reasoned that probably only a few children drowned each year, and the details of each would be kept on a special file in some government office somewhere. The internet, ever-helpful, suggested that INED, the French National Institute for Demographic

Studies, held the answers. Its switchboard operator was unhelpful.

'You want to find out what? How many boys aged thirteen drowned during the last twenty years?'

'Yes,' I confirmed uncertainly, suddenly struck by the hopelessness of the task. During the telling pause that followed I could see clearly in my mind's eye the first of what were to be many Gallic shrugs and upward eye-rolls. Then the receptionist's voice, emotionless apart from a small quaver of disbelief, asked me to wait a moment. I was rapidly transferred, presumably to her least favourite department.

I put my question to a new woman, and was met by the same discouraging silence, followed by a very definite, 'No, we wouldn't have any details like that.' I realized I had to keep her on the line. It was my first call, and I had to draw it out beyond this curt rejection or I might never have the courage to try again. I quickly told her how my friend had found a bottle containing a very sad letter and we wanted to trace the author. In spite of herself the lady began to sound interested, although not optimistic. 'Oh, la la la la la la,' she trilled discouragingly. 'You will never find her.' I told her a little more, about the lock of hair, the boy drifting towards the rising sun. In spite of herself the woman, who sounded young, was intrigued. I told her all I knew, and she began to warm to the challenge. She promised to see if she could find any useful information for me.

Within three hours I received a two-page email and a six-page fax

39

from her about further sources of information. She had even spent some time surfing the internet in search of any references in the press but, like me, had not found anything. Nevertheless I felt I had made some progress.

The official information was potentially useful. She had checked the Statistics for Medical Causes of Death by Drowning. According to the tenth edition of the International Classification of Diseases (CIM), drowning is a disease and the code for this method of dying is E984. Unfortunately her data only went up to 1996 but the total number of boys drowned in France between the ages of ten and fourteen years, for this and the previous five years, was as follows:

1996: 7

1995: 3

1994: 9

1993: 7

1992: 7

1991: 8

She also told me that in a study carried out in 1995, 90 per cent of drownings happened during the months of July or August, and 86.1 per cent occurred in the sea. She referred me to another government statistical institution that, she assured me, could provide more details.

40

In America, drowning is the fourth leading cause of accidental death, claiming 4,000 lives each year, one-third of whom are children under the age of fourteen; and for children under the age of fifteen, drowning claims the second-highest number of lives. That works out at 1,333 children drowned each year, which is proportionately far more than the French figures I had been given. Something seemed out of kilter here.

I had no way of telling whether Maurice had drowned in France, or even within the last decade, but I tried not to think about that. I was encouraged by the woman's response to my plea for information. Although she obviously thought the case hopeless, she was touched by the story. And if a government bureaucrat's heart could be stirred to spend several hours on the search, then it was not just my friend the dog-walker and me, two sentimental and over-imaginative mothers, who found the letter moving. The call to INED had been the very first step in my quest, and although I was in reality no further forward, the official's sympathy had provided me with a much-needed moment of encouragement before embarking on an uncharted sea of unforgiving statistics. The story of Maurice was not just a private obsession, it had a more universal resonance, and if this woman's reaction was symptomatic of what I would come across in my search, then others would be equally helpful. The case, though undeniably tricky, was well on its way to being solved.

The next institution, INSERM (National Institute of Health and Medical Research), dealt in more detail with the same statistics. However, it seemed that the INED figures for drownings of young boys – those aged between ten and fourteen – were only those which were classified as E984 ('Undetermined'); in other words, those deaths that could not be classed as E910 ('Accidental drowning and submersion'), E954 ('Suicide and self-inflicted injury by submersion') or E964 ('Assault by submersion'). The total number of drownings per region was in fact much higher, although it was still substantially lower than in America. The INSERM official kindly sent me the figures for all drownings, whether accidental, self-inflicted or by assault, which added up to between seven and fifty-one per year, and also broke the figures down into regional totals, which provided overall totals of between one and thirty-nine per year for each region of France. None of the figures from one graph seemed to tally with the others, and I was engulfed in a flood of statistics. But the overall message was clear. There were a reasonably large number of boys drowned each year in France and when I added up the numbers over the past twenty years, this amounted to a significant figure.

Death by drowning of boys aged between 10 and 14 years

Years	E910	E954	E964	E984
1979	39	0	0	9
1980	39	0	0	11
1981	29	0	0	17
1982	25	1	0	8
1983	36	1	0	5
1984	28	0	0	17
1985	16	0	1	19
1986	11	1	0	11
1987	24	0	0	9
1988	11	0	0	8
1989	19	1	1	8
1990	14	0	1	8
1991	9	0	0	8
1992	9	0	0	7
1993	6	0	0	7
1994	12	0	0	9
1995	11	0	0	3
1996	13	0	0	7
1997	8	0	1	4
1998	6	0	1	4
1999	1	0	0	6

E910 Accidental drowning and submersion

E954 Suicide and self-inflicted injury by submersion (drowning)

E964 Assault by submersion (drowning)

E984 Submersion (drowning), undetermined whether accidentally or purposely inflicted

Death by drowning and accidental submersion of boys aged between 10 and 14 years

Regions	'79	'80	'81	'82	'83	'84	'85	'86	'87	'88	'89	'90	'91	'92	'93	'94	'95	'96	'97	'98	'99
Ile De France	1	6	1	4	4	4	1	1	5	1	2	2	1	0	0	1	1	1	2	2	0
Champagne-Ardenne	0	1	1	0	0	0	0	0	0	0	0	0	1	0	0	0	0	2	0	0	0
Picardie	2	1	2	1	2	2	1	0	1	0	0	0	0	1	2	2	0	1	0	0	0
Haute-Normandie	1	1	0	1	3	0	0	0	0	0	1	0	1	0	0	0	0	0	1	0	0
Centre	5	3	2	0	0	2	0	0	0	1	0	0	0	1	0	0	1	1	0	1	0
Basse-Normandie	1	1	2	1	1	2	0	0	0	2	1	0	0	0	0	0	2	0	0	0	0
Bourgogne	3	1	1	2	0	1	1	1	2	2	1	1	0	0	0	0	0	0	0	0	0
Nord-Pas-De-Calais	1	2	3	4	3	1	1	0	3	0	3	2	4	0	0	0	2	0	0	1	0
Lorraine	3	1	2	1	1	0	1	2	1	0	0	2	1	1	0	0	1	1	0	0	0
Alsace	5	2	0	0	2	1	1	1	0	0	0	0	0	0	0	3	0	1	1	0	0
Franche-Comte	1	2	1	0	4	1	2	0	1	0	3	0	1	0	1	0	0	0	0	0	0
Pays De Loire	3	0	1	3	2	4	1	1	0	2	0	1	0	1	1	0	0	0	2	1	0
Bretagne	5	3	3	2	3	2	2	2	1	0	1	1	0	1	1	1	1	0	0	0	0
Poitou – Charentes	0	0	1	2	2	0	0	0	4	0	1	0	0	0	0	0	1	0	1	0	0
Aquitaine	2	5	1	2	0	2	1	1	0	0	1	2	0	0	0	0	0	0	0	0	0
Midi-Pyrénées	1	0	2	0	0	0	3	0	3	0	2	1	0	1	0	0	0	0	0	0	0
Limousin	0	0	0	0	0	0	0	0	0	0	0	0	0	0	0	1	0	0	0	0	0
Rhône-Alpes	1	1	3	0	4	1	0	0	0	0	1	0	0	1	0	0	0	2	0	0	1
Auvergne	0	2	0	0	1	1	0	0	1	0	0	0	0	1	0	0	0	0	0	0	0
Languedoc-Roussillon	1	6	2	2	2	1	1	2	1	1	1	0	0	0	0	0	1	1	0	0	0
Prov.-Alpes-côtes-d'azur	3	1	1	0	2	2	0	0	1	0	0	0	0	0	0	2	0	1	1	0	0
Corse	0	0	0	0	0	1	0	0	0	0	0	0	0	0	0	0	0	0	0	0	0
Hors-Métropole	0	0	0	0	0	0	0	0	0	1	2	1	1	1	1	2	1	1	1	1	0
	39	39	29	25	36	28	16	11	24	11	19	14	9	9	6	12	11	13	8	6	1

The most serious flaw in my methodology, however, was that neither the lady from INED nor the lady from INSERM believed that it would be possible to track these statistics back to the individuals concerned.

I rang the British Foreign Office because I was trying to understand how the French bureaucracy dealt with death. Its filtering system was immaculate, and I failed to penetrate beyond assistant level in the department dealing with Deaths Abroad. However, the assistant was able to supply me with a list of undertakers specializing in international repatriation from France. I decided to settle for that.

The receptionist at the international undertakers was very forthcoming, and told me that when her company repatriated a corpse from France the job details were handled by the insurance company or by the French undertakers. The main French company's representative, a very practical, direct man who spoke extraordinarily fast French, explained patiently that coroners did not exist in France, contrary to the advice of my dictionary, which translated coroner as 'coroner', presumably with a rolled 'r' and a rising inflection at the end. This explained why everyone I had so far interrogated had been completely mystified by my use of the term. Instead, he assured me, the police or the gendarmerie would file an initial report on a suspicious death for the Procureur de la République, the Public Prosecutor of that particular town or region. The Procureur would then decide whether to give permission for burial, or request a further investigation. The Procureur's files are not open to the public; not even the undertaker is allowed to know the details of the death of its clients. The death certificate, he told me, is then kept on file at the town hall. There are some 36,000 individual communities, with their own town halls, throughout France and he laughed uproariously at the thought that I hoped to track down a thirteen-year-old boy with only a first name via this method. His laughter would return to haunt me during the months of research that followed.

When I reviewed my progress after the morning's telephone calls, I realized that apart from learning that there was no such thing as a coroner in France, I had succeeded only in making a fool of myself.

Despite the absence of a coroner in the French system, I contacted one in London to find out about the procedure following death in France. An officer readily and helpfully explained that he often had to deal with deaths of UK citizens abroad, so he knew a little about it. He confirmed that there were no coroners in France, but rather an examining magistrate, the Procureur. He said that the French carried out far fewer autopsies and investigated incidents less thoroughly than in the UK. He then paused and added as an afterthought that perhaps the English investigate things too thoroughly. Anyhow, he was happy to show me a file dealing with a death in France, so that I could familiarize myself with the process and note any useful addresses and terminology. I thought it would provide a gentle introduction to the subject, a springboard from which to leap into unknown waters, so I accepted his invitation to come in and talk about the matter further.

Coroner's officers, many of them retired policemen, seem to run the system, ensuring that the relevant paperwork is available for cases to be settled efficiently. I was shown into a nondescript office in central London by the officer I had come to meet, who fitted the image of a coroner perfectly. He pulled out a large atlas; I took out a translation of the letter in the bottle. The document itself was too florally written for his taste, and I could see his eyes glaze over while he was still perusing the first paragraph. But he was clearly intrigued by my quest. Standing over a map of the Kent coast and the English Channel, the officer wondered aloud how a bottle could wash up on such an unlikely beach, not directly opposite France and sheltered from the main tidal sweep. 'Of all the deaths I've had to deal with all over the world,' he said, 'this is the most puzzling.' Usually he had to assess police files and medical reports. All I had was a naked letter, unsupported by a body or any official apparatus. Perhaps it was the sheer hopelessness that was attractive to a professional used to organizing proper quantities of evidence and facts.

Karen Liebreich

The case he was dealing with at that moment involved a road accident in France. A couple on a motorbike had been hit by someone speeding on the motorway. The woman had been killed, her husband had been thrown clear and was only slightly injured. The story of the driver who had collided with them conflicted with the versions provided by all the other witnesses, while the poor husband had seen nothing until the car hit him and his wife from the rear. Searching through the file, trying to look only for useful information, I nevertheless found myself caught up in their tragedy. A bright summer's day, the promise of a holiday, a moment of stupidity by a young man they had never met, and lives shattered.

In France, the officer explained, the police prepared a dossier about a death and sent it to the Public Prosecutor, Monsieur le Procureur de la République, who decided on the basis of the evidence whether to proceed with a full investigation, or whether to permit a death certificate to be sent on to the Mayor's office. This confirmed what the French undertaker had told me.

But I had no idea whether Maurice's death had been judged worthy of further investigation.

6

I had never had occasion to use the services of a private detective, although I had often seen their adverts in local papers. I had even thought of it as a possible career avenue, a kind of natural progression from the kind of academic research I did for a living. Once an American company had asked me to check out one of their employees in London and I had speedily discovered that not only had he failed to direct the films and television programmes he listed on his CV, but he was not a director of the Natural History Museum as he claimed. Moreover, he was a bankrupt with two court judgements against him, and also a bigamist with a wife in Richmond, Surrey, and another in California. Ever since then I had thought that if I was short of work, I could probably turn my hand to private detecting.

But now I felt in need of reinforcements. In novels, private detectives always have good connections with the regular police force so that they can access their national databases. It seemed to me that if I could find a helpful private eye, I could circumvent a good deal of time-wasting. With one telephone call he would organize it all. Perhaps it would take a little longer, since there was an international angle; perhaps he would call his man in Paris. Perhaps he had a contact at Interpol. In my inner heart I knew that it was unlikely to be that simple, but there was a chance that it could provide a short cut. And anyhow, I had always wanted to visit a private detective.

The advert promised 'Private, Matrimonial, Commercial & Civil. All forms of enquiries undertaken with discretion and sensitivity'. The person at the end of the phone was initially dismissive, then intrigued. It was a reaction I had by now come to expect. My reluctance to fax the letter to the detective made him even more curious. Eventually we agreed to meet. He assured me that there would be no charge; he would work *pro bono*, out of pure 'intellectual curiosity'. I was beginning to realize that detecting must have its dull moments and that my enquiry had touched a chord of curiosity here as elsewhere.

The office was perfectly situated between the council estates and prison at Wormwood Scrubs and the wealthy and fashionable clientele of Notting Hill and Portobello Road. I had initially spoken to the junior partner, but when I arrived I found that the chief investigator had decided to take up the case in person. His room was splendid, a temple to Raymond Chandler and Dashiell Hammett. It contained a large wooden desk, a massive old metal safe in the corner, a huge maroon winged leather armchair, a framed letter of thanks with an old-fashioned magnifying glass suspended over the most important phrases in the letter, a large round fishbowl with two healthy-looking fish circling around, a detailed map of London and a certificate from the World Association of Detectives. Only the laptop was anachronistic. He gestured me towards the armchair and as I sank into it I realized that it was so deep I couldn't reach the back without slumping clumsily or sticking out my legs in front of me. I perched on the edge and wished I had worn a pencil skirt, a short black veil, teetering heels and crimson lipstick.

Not sure what to say, I remarked that the chair was just right for the job. The investigator smiled. 'It has seen many tears, that chair.' I was delighted. He was in his mid-forties, fair-haired with a dark jacket and trousers, and unnervingly grey-white shoes – glamorous but slightly dilapidated. He had started in the business twenty-six years ago, first working for a debt-tracing agency, and had then specialized in asset identification, providing information for debt collectors, before setting up the current company. He took the English translation of the letter and began to pore over it at the same time as devouring a huge bowl of muesli. I was enchanted.

He explained that this case was very different from his usual line of business. During our meeting a potential client telephoned about having his ex-girlfriend followed. Was she seeing someone else? the detective asked. Why had she ended the relationship? This was clearly a bread-and-butter case for him and he handled it with weary efficiency.

He read the letter slowly and thoroughly, querying the nuances in my translation throughout. As he revealed the discrepancies in my initial hasty effort, I resolved to call a literary French friend and check every syllable. He showed no visible emotional reaction and made no personal comments. The letter was like a crossword to be deciphered for clues; nothing further. In my initial reading, the only real clues had been the name of the child and his age. But the investigator chewed over other angles, as he digested his muesli. Breakfast ended with a handful of pills, all washed down by one efficient swallow of water. Maurice was the first son, he noted. Had he been lost in a storm? 'S'est dérobé à la vie' – 'slipped away from life' but literally 'unclothed himself of life'. Had he let it slide from his shoulders like a bathrobe? Had he taken drugs? Had he committed suicide? Had he simply overestimated his swimming or sailing abilities? 'Forgive me for being so angry at your disappearance', literally 'the anger that was your disappearance'. Had mother and son had a huge row, after which he had swum away to his death? Had his body been missing for a while? He had drifted ashore close to the rising sun, so to the east.

Had I contacted the police in Kent, where the bottle had been found? Maybe an ESDA test would throw up some new information. He explained that this meant Electronic Static Detection Analysis and was a special technique that could throw very slight impressions on paper into legible relief. So if, by some miraculous chance, the mother had written her name and address on the page above, the faintest traces might come through the pad to the next page, and an ESDA test might reveal them.

The meeting produced many more questions, and no answers. It was clear that the detective was intrigued, but not so curious that he would offer to answer any of these questions himself *pro bono*. From the tone of his voice, he was not very hopeful of success. Rather than employ him, I decided to follow up his suggestions myself.

The policewoman to whom I spoke when I telephoned the Kent Constabulary was friendly and helpful. Without a name or a date, however, the information they could offer was limited. I was passed from station to station, retelling my tale each time to the duty officer who had been there for the longest period. They were unfailingly polite and curious, but no one could recall any bodies of thirteen-year-old boys washed up on their beaches. I soon began to fret at the amount of police time I was wasting.

The private detective had also provided me with a contact number where I could organize an ESDA test on the paper on which the letter had been written. By then it must have been obvious that I had no funds to pay him for investigative services, and perhaps he realized he had nothing to lose by offering me the details. Routine and dull as it might be, checking up on unfaithful lovers was going to continue paying the bills, whereas I, as he had probably guessed from the start, was on a long quest with no certainty of finding an answer.

There was one very important element that I had not yet considered, though it was potentially full of clues: the bottle. The choice of vessel, its origin, its image, its date of manufacture – all this information could be of use. I decided to ring the mineral water company, Evian.

It was obvious from the most cursory research on the internet that Evian belonged to the Danone Corporation. The English headquarters promised to call back with information on the bottle but did not, so I decided to ring the '24-hour Evian telephone consumer service'. 'Delphine' took the call but was, perhaps understandably, reluctant to listen to the details. It was far removed from the kind of questioning for which she had been trained, and I was not interested in how many years the water had been filtered 'through pristine glacial rock formations in the French Alps'. It turned out to be fifteen years.

She was inclined to be dismissive of my query, but when I

persisted, describing the beauty of the bottle, she told me that this type of container had first been released in limited numbers for the Albertville Winter Olympic Games of 1992. Its success was such that it was relaunched as the Millennium Bottle in late 1999. According to the company website, 'This pure and perfect form is the very symbol of water.' Since then, by public demand, it had been re-released every year. As many as 400,000 of these bottles were in circulation. I mentioned that the one in question had 20-02 engraved on it. Wouldn't that narrow down the field? She conceded the point, though somewhat reluctantly.

No, I could not bring the bottle in to ask for any more information. No, visitors were not allowed at the Evian factory. I pointed out that I was not attacking Evian; on the contrary, someone had thought their bottle a suitable vessel for the most important letter of her life. Finally she agreed to pass the message upwards and promised me that someone would return my call.

The Director of External Relations for Danone rang back and left a message on my machine. 'We are not particularly interested in your little story of a bottle on the beach,' she said in a tone of the most superior scorn and disdain. 'But if you want to ring me, I'm on . . . ' and she rattled off a number full of reversed 80s and 90s in the speediest French possible, which took me eighteen message replays to decipher. Four-twenty-five, four-twenty-eleven, fifty-two, four-twenty-ten-seven, twenty-six, four-twenty-five, four-twenty-eleven, fifty-two, four-twenty-ten-seven, twenty-six. Finally I worked out that she had repeated her number twice on the message but without drawing breath in between. I gritted my teeth and realized I had to try to win her over in order to secure vital clues about the bottle.

At a drinks party for affluent London bankers to which my partner and I had been invited because our sons were friendly, I talked to a glamorous woman about my search. 'What a wonderful idea,' she cried. It was as though I had declared my intention to take up embroidery or charity work. 'But it's really very simple. My husband is a stockbroker and he has access to a wonderful database of all the news in the world.' She obviously believed that her husband solved the problems of world finance at the touch of a keyboard, well before the FTSE 100 even opened each day. 'You can just type your clues in and he will find the result for you in no time at all.'

My first reaction was one of irritation at her calm assumption of her husband's superiority – or the superiority of his technology over my more pedestrian research methods. Then I decided instead to be delighted. If I took advantage of the offer, my search would very soon be over. I could draw a line under this increasingly ridiculous episode, and get on with my life once again. The questions that had begun to niggle at me whenever I tried to do something else, like irritating mosquito bites that must be scratched, would be assuaged. I would know who the mother was and how the boy had died. I supplied the stockbroker's wife with the scarce details: the boy was called Maurice and he was thirteen when he drowned at the dawn of summer. Her immaculate smile became a little strained when she realized quite how sparse the information was, but she gamely noted it down in a tiny mother-of-pearl notebook to pass on to her husband at a more appropriate time.

Two weeks later, I received a brief email from her. 'Unfortunately, my husband's research yielded rubbish. A little more information is necessary.' Despite my disappointment, I somehow felt relieved that the secrets could not be extracted at the press of an internet button. The world's search engines and its financial, commercial and legal databases could not just spit out the answer in an insulting fraction of a second.

I spent several days composing an eloquent email to convince the spokesperson at Evian to talk to me. I finally sent it on a Friday evening, hoping that on Monday morning she would read it and find it irresistible. But all that weekend I watched news coverage of the G8 meeting in Evian and the anti-globalization campaigners rioting in the streets of the nearby towns. Even if Madame had managed to get to work unruffled, she would probably be feeling unsympathetic towards Anglo-Saxon time-wasters.

To my astonishment she rang first thing on Monday and left a message in English. It turned out that she spoke it perfectly. I was thrilled. I rang back and we had a long chat about the development of bottle design. This particular bottle, the 'Evian Millennium 2002', had been in production from October 2001. My friend the dog-walker had found the bottle in February 2002, some four months later. Finally I had a real fact to grasp in an ocean of conjecture and supposition. The bottle had been cast into the sea between October 2001 and 17 February 2002.

It was likely that the day matched the bleakness of the mother's mood, with an unfriendly sea, where 'restlesse mindes are tossed'. Perhaps it was grey and stormy, but with a hint of spring to come. A slight lightening of the sky, reflected in the 'I'm doing better now, my love' of the letter, and the comfort of friendship alluded to in the closing lines.

The woman at Evian then unwittingly supplied me with another concrete piece of information. We were getting on so well that I decided to read her the opening lines of the letter. She interrupted me and said, 'You know, that sounds just like the Kevin Costner film

Message in a Bottle.' I humoured her – after all, her co-operation was important – pointing out that this story is true tragedy while that one is just Hollywood fantasy. She insisted that the film was very similar and started to tell me the plot; it sounded very convoluted, with as many deaths as *Hamlet*. Battered into reluctant submission, I agreed to watch the film, and she in return agreed that I could come and visit the factory if I wanted to, an offer she would later rescind. Meanwhile she made a note to send me a press pack that, she assured me, would contain absolutely nothing of any use.

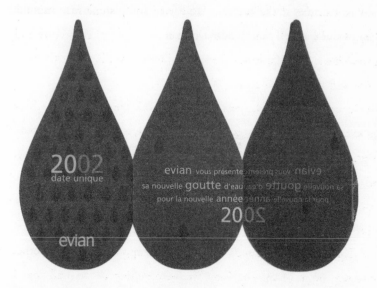

I now knew that the bottle had been manufactured only a few months before it had been found, so it had not been floating towards us for years. I knew the numbers of boys drowned in the previous decades but was apparently unable to track down the individuals from the national statistical databases. I knew that the police, the coroners' service and the Foreign Office were unable to advance the search. And I knew a little more about the history of the strange method of communication through letters in bottles. But I still had no idea who the mother was, who the son was, or why or how he had died.

My friend the dog-walker was surprised that I was still bothering. But I was hooked, as much by pure curiosity or out of sympathy as by irritation at my failure thus far. I felt I still had many more angles to pursue before I had to admit defeat.

7

I rented *Message in a Bottle* from the local video store. I knew it existed and had in fact thought of taking it out a few weeks earlier, but the cover portrayed an image so syrupy that I had decided I simply couldn't face Kevin Costner's heartbreak. However, I had assured the woman from Evian that I would watch the film and so, in the hope that it would yield some useful information, I steeled myself to do so.

Divorcee journalist Theresa, played by Robin Wright Penn, is jogging along the beach when she stumbles across a bottle with a message. She shows the letter around the newspaper office where she works and her editor, played by Robbie Coltrane, publishes it without her prior knowledge. The newspaper's 'research department' tells the journalist that the typewriter used to write the letter is probably five years old; the cork has been in the water only two years. The letter is published and two more letters on identical stationery are received from readers. Theresa reads out the third letter:

'To all the ships at sea and all the ports of call, to my family and to all friends and strangers.'

I had been lounging comfortably, glass of wine in hand, gently revelling in the guilt-free sensation of watching a schlock film in the interests of research when the phrase hit me like a cold wave. My drink spilt as I almost fell out of my armchair.

'This is a message, a prayer. The message is that my travels taught me a great truth. I already had what everyone is searching for and few ever find: the one person in the world whom I was born to love forever . . . The prayer is that everyone in the world can know this kind of love and be healed by it. If my prayer is heard there will be an erasing of all guilt and all regret and an end to all anger. Please God. Amen.'

Somehow Hollywood had got hold of my letter. I felt a mixture of outrage at the invasion, triumph at having tracked down at least a part of the letter's source, and horror that the opening lines of my letter had been plagiarized.

I wound and rewound my VCR to take a note of the words, before running to compare them with my letter in a bottle. Just as when I discovered from Evian that the bottle had only been in the water for a maximum of four months, so I now felt I had made a real leap forward in understanding my letter-writer. Now I knew that she had definitely watched this film, and that it had had a great impact on her. On the other hand, my search felt just a little tarnished. The opening lines of her letter were not original, though the translation into French and back again had introduced some small differences. But neither was my search original. I was simply recreating the clichéd tale of a best-selling novel and its film adaptation.

Theresa, aided by her 'research department', manages to track down the paper on which the letter was written within the next two minutes. If only my letter-writer had supplied a clue as to her location. Or if only I had access to such an effective 'research department'. The other main difference between my 'real' letter and the filmic one is that the object of her love is her son, not her lover. And that my letter-writer is real. I think. Apart from the opening paragraph, and a little extract at the end, that are taken from the film, she writes her own letter. I think.

I watched the rest of the film in an excited but confused state. Theresa, the journalist, travels to the Outer Banks in North Carolina where she meets Kevin Costner. Inevitably they fall in love. Theresa finds it impossible to tell him the truth of how she came to find him, fearing his reaction. Of course Costner eventually discovers the deception, opening her bedside drawer and finding the letters he had thrown into the sea after the death of his wife two years earlier. Theresa had balked at the ethical dilemma involved in finding a letter in a bottle, tracking down the sender and then falling in love and sleeping with him. I can sympathize with the first two elements of her equation. I justify it by telling myself that the mother – just as the writer in the film – addressed her letter 'To all ships at sea, to all ports of call, to my family, to all friends and strangers.' Sending a letter in a bottle invites a stranger to pick it up and read it. By definition, a letter broadcast to the waves and addressed to the whole world can no longer be private. Somehow I think the unknown mother wanted the tale of her love for her son, the knowledge of his death and her despair, to be known. Where the journalist in the film erred was in deceiving Costner, afraid to tell him about the letters at first, then becoming emotionally involved and afraid of his reaction. I felt I could not lie to my letter-writer, if I ever found her.

Costner runs from Theresa's apartment into the pouring rain, pursued by her apologizing and explaining. As they shout at one another in the downpour it becomes clear that Costner only wrote two letters, but the journalist has found three; the letter from which the unknown mother lifted a paragraph was written not by Costner, but by Costner's wife. Her last action was to rise from her deathbed, type out this letter, totter to the cliffs in her billowing white night-dress, and hurl the bottle into the sea, before falling back unconscious into her husband's arms. You have to be in the right mood to find this anything but embarrassingly corny. Anyhow, Costner still adores his wife and is finding it hard to let himself love Theresa, but his father, played by Paul Newman, tells him that he has to choose between yesterday and tomorrow. He writes yet another letter and slips it into the pocket of his waterproofs, but is drowned while heroically saving a family from a sinking yacht before he can send it. Luckily he stripped off the waterproofs before diving into the sea, so the last letter he wrote is found and returned to his father and Theresa. The film closes with Theresa walking alone on the beach and her voice-over saying: 'If some lives form a perfect circle, others take shape in ways we cannot predict or always understand. Loss has been a part of my journey but it has also shown me what is precious. So has a love for which I can only be grateful.' My letter-writer had cannibalized these words too.

The mother must have seen this film and been moved by it. It was released in 1999. The accuracy of her quotation indicates that she had made a considerable effort with these lines. She either replayed it endlessly on video or DVD while she copied them out, or she watched the film so many times that she knew it by heart. Either way, it was strangely moving that this somewhat far-fetched love story had made such an impact on a lonely woman.

Or could the whole thing be a hoax? No, I think that a practical joker would have left some method by which he or she could have measured the success of the joke, in other words a return address. And more crucially than that, I think the emotions are too raw and sincere, and the subject too bleak, for a prankster.

I wondered if she had also seen *Castaway*, in which Tom Hanks's character, Chuck Nolan (No-land), gradually discovers that 'you never know what the tide will bring'. Or another Costner film, *Waterworld*, set 'within a vast sphere, ever drifting in uncertainty, driven from end to end'. Given her familiarity with Costner's later film, it is quite likely. I asked myself whether the woman brooded over her son's death until this film inspired her to write her letter and consign it to the waves? Or did the idea hit her immediately as she watched the film?

Message in a Bottle does not have a conventional happy ending. Like the letter-writer's story, it ends in grief but also in a certain acceptance of death, and a forgiveness of earlier errors. The heroine is alone on a beach at the beginning, and alone once again on a beach at the end, but in between she has experienced great love. The cliché 'Better to have loved and lost than never to have loved at all' is vindicated and she walks off into the sunset, alone but no longer lonely.

I wept in spite of myself, not so much because I was caught up in Theresa's experience, but at the thought of the unknown mother's grief and empathy as she watched this. When I first heard those lines from the letter in the film, I was appalled that the poetic figure of my imagination, the woman who had written so lyrically and heart-rendingly of her loss, had suddenly metamorphosed into a fan of Hollywood slush. Or that it might mean the whole letter was a figment of someone's overblown sense of drama or humour. But then I realized that I still believed in the letter's authenticity, I was still convinced that it represented a real tragedy, and that the letter was not tarnished by her plagiarism. Rather, it emphasized our common cultural background. She may be a Frenchwoman with a poetic turn of phrase and a tragic past, but she still watched romantic Hollywood films like the rest of us.

'The attractions, fascinations there are in sea and shore! How one dwells on their simplicity, even vacuity! What is it in us, arous'd by those indirections and directions? That spread of waves and gray-white beach, salt, monotonous, senseless – such an entire absence of art, books, talk, elegance – so inde-scribably comforting, even this winter day – grim, yet so delicate-looking, so spiritual – striking emotional, impalpable depths, subtler than all the paintings, music, I have ever read, seen, heard. (Yet let me be fair, perhaps it is because I have read those poems and heard that music.)'

Walt Whitman, 'A Winter Day on the Sea-Beach', 1882

Or seen that film.

8

So far I had carried out my enquiries in England, either by telephone or by visiting people such as the coroner or the private detective. It was obvious that I would have to return to France to continue my search. It was beginning to be a more serious investigation. I decided to concentrate my initial researches on finding any mention of the death of Maurice in the local papers for the northern coastal region. It seemed to me that the death of a thirteen-year-old by drowning was worthy of either a small article or a notification of bereavement. Like the births, deaths and marriages sections in *The Times*, people pay to include details of the passing of their loved ones, and I thought the death of a much-loved child might well have merited one of the black-bordered notices that are common throughout most of Europe even though they are almost unknown in the United Kingdom.

The best way to search for these notices, I was assured by several librarians and archivists, was to visit the Bibliothèque nationale de France based in Paris. There I would find all the regional journals and newspapers and would be able to narrow down my search accurately.

It was August 2003 and Europe was roasting in the hottest summer on record. Throughout France, the elderly were dying in their apartments. Later the French press would blame the younger generation for abandoning their old relations to spend the summer by the sea. During the first two weeks of the month 15,000 deaths above the usual level of mortality were recorded. Paris felt empty, broiled and alien. The strangeness of the city added to the feeling that now that I had left my own country my quest was entering a more significant stage.

The library is one of François Mitterrand's 'grands projets' and is situated in the 13th arrondissement, an area where abandoned warehouses are being converted for other use or knocked down. It sits in the midst of its own sea of sun-broiled ipê decking, a Brazilian hardwood. There is no shelter or shade on the approaches to the building – the small bushy trees on the edges of the decking are encased in wire grilles, to prevent birds from building nests that would ruin the architectural lines. A library leaflet claims it is the emptiness – 'le vide'– that arrests the attention and the vast sweep of space around the library is indeed impressive in its sterility. An insect trying to crawl across the decking would have fried within seconds. Later I was told that summer was the best season to visit the library, for when it rains the surface is lethally slippery and in winter the open space between the towers is transformed into a bleak and hostile wind tunnel. Signs showing falling stick figures warn against the treacherous nature of all the access routes, decking and moving escalators.

There are four glass towers, designed to represent four open books, linking sky and soil. The architect, Gilles Perrault, saw them as silos, 'whose grains will be the books summoned downwards to meet their readers'. They are evocatively named – Time, Laws, Letters and Numbers – with the restricted-access collection of pornography called l'Enfer, Hell. The architect intended the glass of the towers to be photochromatic, but the budget ran out, and when, belatedly, it occurred to someone that glass was not the most suitable material to protect light-sensitive books, shutters were added. The resulting impression is that of a derelict office block.

Sunk into the centre of the decking, with the towers sticking up like a dead dog's legs at each corner, is a pit containing a small forest. Twenty mature silver pines weighing twelve tons each were dug up from an ancient Norman forest to create this 'sacred garden', which readers can see from the surrounding subterranean reading room but may not touch. The trees with their inadequate root-runs are restrained by metal guy ropes.

71

The library seems to represent an attempt at absolute domination of nature by man with its use of wood as decking, the caged saplings outside, and the transplanted and chained tree trunks in this tiny forest. And the treacherous slickness of the wet decking and the biting winds in winter, or the shadeless heat and the damaging rays of sun through the glass towers in summer, seem to be nature's way of fighting back.

Over-size steel doors guard a long escalator that descends into a bunker clad in steel webbing, resembling the final destination in a *Terminator* film. The experience of researching at this library seemed designed to create the impression of a complete break with any external reality. It seemed appropriate to my mission. After all, I was leaving my own family to hunt for traces of a dead child in this strange mausoleum of a library.

I decided to begin my search at the bibliographic enquiry desk. The introductory leaflet encouragingly noted that this was 'the best room to start your research – or to decide not to continue with it'. I explained in French to the assistant who resembled a squatting toad, bristling with a sullen lack of expression, that I was looking for local newspaper reports of a boy who had drowned. She looked doubtful so I explained about the letter. When she was still unimpressed, I pulled out a copy and watched her read it. She scanned through the letter, clicking her tongue disapprovingly and shaking her head, and told me I was wasting my time without checking the tidal patterns and carrying out psychiatric reports on the subject. After a forty-five-minute discussion she suddenly asked me, 'Do you *speak* French?' I stared at her in outrage. How had we just been communicating?

'Well, to a Francophone this letter means so much more,' she explained. 'This phrase, for instance,' and she gestured contemptuously at the lines, *Today the journey is ending, my son has reached harbour again* . . . 'This is just so banal. It's completely useless. You really are wasting your time. You have to have a plan of research – and even then, what a waste of time.' Her words ground away at my

73

optimism and self-confidence. Concealing my exasperation, I asked if she could simply let me know the names of the regional newspapers for each of the areas along the north coast of France. She continued to pore over the letter, and in an effort to prove that I had already discovered something of great relevance, I foolishly told her about the link with the film.

'A woman who would watch that kind of film,' she stated categorically, 'might well travel quite a distance to throw a bottle into the sea, so there's no point looking in the regional papers.'

But finally, witheringly, she pulled out a local press directory, and as she was distracted by a telephone call, I pulled it over and copied out the details as fast as I could. By the time she returned I had nearly finished. As I turned to go I asked whether, in spite of her scepticism, she would like to know how I got on. She spun her revolving chair round with surprising eagerness and snatched up a piece of scrap paper. 'I'll give you my email address,' she answered.

My confidence was at its lowest ebb. The librarian's helpfulness had been overlaid with such condescension that I had doubts about my motivation and also about the ethics of my search. Had she not already ordered enough local newspapers to keep me busy for the foreseeable future, I would probably have given up right there. But the message soon arrived that my material was ready for consultation, and having travelled so far I decided to continue with my original plan of research. I would read all the local papers for the northern coast of France, starting from the west in Brittany and working towards the east, through Normandy towards Calais. I would concentrate on the early summer months, since the mother mentioned 'the dawn of summer' as the time of death. She also wrote, 'Forgive me, my son for not having spoken to you for such a long time'; I concluded from this that she had been unable to express her emotions for a few years after his death so it had taken her some time to be able to put pen to paper. This seemed more likely than the alternative explanation that she had been unable to speak to her son properly for several years before he died.

So I decided to start my hunt in the month of June, five years before the bottle's discovery. I was not entirely convinced of my logic, but faced with such a daunting prospect I could either go back home to London, tail between my legs, or simply start somewhere, and hope to strike paydirt.

To my dismay, the first of the newspapers, *Ouest France*, arrived on microfilm. I threaded up my machine and wound slowly through the issues, searching for the page of death notices. The Maurices were all very ancient. Monsignor Maurice Chatillon, an Honorary Vicar General, was 97; Maurice Rob, an ancient soldier of the Second World War, was 78; Maurice Lemaire was 92. This covered all the Maurices for June 1995.

After *Ouest France* I turned to *Paris-Normandie*, and then to *Nord-Éclair*. By the time I had spooled through these three newspapers for each of the thirty daily editions of June 1995 my eyes were dimming and my gorge rising with nausea. It was impossible to wind the microfilm any faster and still scan the articles and locate the obituary page; the floor of my booth was already tilting alarmingly, and I knew I could not continue in this way. It would be physically impossible to skim several decades of newspaper obituaries on microfilm. The decision had been taken out of my hands.

The last newspaper I wanted to consult was *La Voix du Nord*. To my relief, it was available in hard copy. It covered the two French regions closest to the English beach on which the bottle had been found, Pas de Calais and Nord. By now dusk was falling, so I ordered up all the editions for the month of June from 1995 to 2000 for the following day.

The August heat in Paris was blistering. I was staying in a flat near the Eiffel Tower. Each morning, after a sleepless night, I would walk through the empty streets, enter an airless metro, traverse the building site where the surrounding industrial wasteland was being transformed into gingko-fringed boulevards, cross the Brazilian ipê decking cooking like Saint Laurence on his gridiron, and enter the glass-and-steel bunker of the library to immerse myself in the sad banality of death in the French provinces.

I was allocated a large lectern on which to consult my newspapers. *La Voix du Nord* – *le grand quotidien d'information*, 'the great news daily' – is a broadsheet. As the hours passed, I became adept at turning the pages swiftly to the 'Nécrologie' and skimming through the names and ages, in search of Maurice, aged thirteen.

I read the names and professions quietly to myself to stay awake – Bernard, Emile, André, Clorinthe (retired), Cécile, Jean, Madeleine, Joseph (gardener and florist), Marthe (hairdresser), Léon, Solange, Antoinette, Paul, Jules, Patrick, Onéphyle (market gardener) . . . The poesy of the names lulled me into a rhythmic rocking, like an old Jew at prayer, and I wondered if, in my trance-like state, I would even remember that I was searching for a Maurice if ever I should stumble across one.

There were so many young deaths that caught at my heart. There were the mothers who 'after a long illness' left their partners with small children to cope alone. There was Karine who died in June 1997, but even by June 2001 her family were still not coming to terms with their loss. The notice read:

It has now been four years, it should be getting better.

Well, it's not getting better. It's getting worse and worse.

Daughter of nowhere, she could not find her place in this intolerant world.

She could not cope with the brutal death of her Daddy.

Through her Art she expressed her priorities: Love, Happiness, Freedom . . .

For four years, for those who really loved her in all her mystery, her absence remains unbearable, the wound still gapes, especially for her mother and for those closest to her.

A picture of a smiling girl in her late teens, head tilted to one side. The raw pain of the message.

But as I worked my way through the Junes of 1995, 1996, 1997, 1998 and 1999 (Maurice Keirsgieter, erstwhile baker and prisoner of war, aged 83), 2000 and 2001, I became more and more convinced that 'the dawn of summer' when Maurice died was in fact May. I ordered up a new batch of *La Voix du Nord.*

I was distracted by a small article on 30 May 2000 about a decision of the administrative Court of Appeal, which decreed that Joëlle and Michel Leroy (Professor of Philosophy, aged 52) could not keep their mother's body in the freezer. Their mother, Lise, had died on 13 July 1999 and although, the article noted, she was paraplegic, she had encouraged both her children to study. They cited as justification for retaining her body the 'very great affection' they felt for her, and were most reluctant to consign her remains to the earth or the furnace, preferring to keep her in the kitchen. Professor Leroy intended to continue his appeal to a higher court, and was particularly disappointed by the decision 'since this news arrives the day after Mother's Day'.

Philogone, Fernand, Fénelon, Claudet, Rémy, Octave, Evariste, Daniel, Anne-Doris, Adalbert . . . Death's harvest was particularly poetic on 3 May 2000. Then there were the regulars, whose families remembered them on the same date each year. Every 11 May, André's family sent in a notice of remembrance of his death, aged 29, cremated according to his wishes in the strictest privacy. Every 28 May Lorenzo and Fabio were mourned: 'Two stars who never stop shining.' A photograph of two boys out for a laugh together, one with his tongue sticking out. A road accident?

The closest in age to the death I was seeking was Jérôme, kung fu vice-champion of France, aged fourteen.

As each edition was searched and discarded I felt the odds narrowing. Surely the next edition would contain the notice I sought. As the pile of papers to be searched shrank my excitement mounted.

All day I sat alone, reading obituaries of small, incomplete lives and the grief they left behind. And in the evening I would re-emerge from the majestic escalators of the library, cross the deserted planks of Mitterrand's folly and dive once more into the métro. Too tired to deviate, too emotionally drained to socialize, I was befuddled by the collective grief of the Pas de Calais region of France.

One evening, dazed by a day trawling through the papers, I went with my Parisian host to visit an artist friend on the outskirts of the city. My existence had shrunk to the metro, the library and the death notices. We sat in the garden, sipping ginger-flavoured lemonade and talking quietly. Bamboo fringed the unkempt lawn, Ladakhi prayer flags fluttered through the foliage, a row of conifers screened off a neighbouring building. In the centre of the grass, under a little palm, sat a stone Vietnamese sage, roughly hewn and coarse but patinated into beauty.

The artist became interested in my search. She told me of her friend, a graphologist, who was known for her intuition and her psychological insights. She told me of another friend, Christine, who read tarot and had uncovered a dark secret about the artist's husband – who had then left her. She told me about an acquaintance who was a 'bulbologue', a follicologist, whose mother had been a hairdresser and who had been fascinated by hair since before he could crawl. A toddlerhood spent at his mother's feet among the shorn curls of her clients had marked him for life, and he had grown up to become a world expert on hair, consulted, she assured me, by Interpol on their most complex cases. She gave me a bright orange notelet with the contact details of all these people.

Depressed by my first ventures into the archives of death, and entranced by the new avenues of research I saw opening up before me, I purchased a painting from the artist. It depicted a mysterious golden globe made up of tiny question marks, afloat in a deep blue sky that stretched back into the textured infinity of the canvas.

As we drove home from the artist's house, my host told me that she too had recently gone to a follicle specialist. He had run his hands through her hair, stopping at certain tufts to exclaim that this strand showed she had been divorced, this thinner patch showed problems at work, and this area above her temple showed that she had lacked a father in her childhood. After this analysis, the accuracy of which had completely amazed and convinced her, he had taken a razor blade and, holding handfuls of her hair firmly outwards from the scalp, had sliced through the taut strands upwards from shoulders to crown, using the tension of the extended hair to dictate the cut. The vibrations caused by this process at the root of each hair, he told her, would liberate her from past traumas. It was, she assured me, excruciatingly painful, and as tears of agony welled in her eyes, the specialist announced that the experiences that blocked her psyche had been cleansed away. The follicles were now purified and reinvigorated, and she would be able to face life afresh.

She recounted the tale with self-deprecating humour, but she – and many of her friends, all university-educated intellectuals teaching at schools or universities or working in the upper levels of the French civil and diplomatic services – paid good money to visit this man and took his predictions and diagnoses seriously. I told myself that while I would be convinced by DNA and scientific analysis of any chemical residues in the hair, I was not going to subject the lock of hair from the letter in the bottle to this kind of psycho-tuft treatment.

9

I returned to England with my new painting under one arm and a folder full of notes on the French regional newspapers under the other. The librarian's comments had stung me and I resolved to continue my research in a more methodical way. Firstly I would reread the letter, check my translation, and try to get some medical opinions about the mental health of the writer. I would also endeavour to find out more about the tide patterns and attempt to identify the point of origin of the bottle. I had had such high hopes of the local papers that I had thought the mystery would be solved by now, without my having to continue with any further research. If necessary, I would then follow up the contact numbers that the artist had given: the follicologist, the graphologist and the tarot reader.

I invited a translator friend to dinner, pointing out that she would have to spend several hours earning her meal by checking my version of the letter. We resolved some ambiguities, although because they were real ambiguities, we simply prioritized one version over the other. For instance, we decided that 's'est dérobé à la vie dans un trop plein de désirs' – 'he slipped away from/shed/escaped from his life in an overflow/surplus/excess of desires' – could best be translated as 'he slipped away from life in an excess of desires'; 'pour tenter d'éteindre infatigablement le repos de ses deux bras tendus' lost all reference to extinguishing indefatigably the rest of his outstretched arms and became 'trying tirelessly to use up the strength in his outstretched arms', although we were not entirely happy with translating 'repos' (rest) as strength.

To my surprise, the friend provided a completely different interpretation of the letter. For her, a gay woman, it was clearly a confession of a long-suppressed sexuality and an explanation to Maurice of the letter-writer's decision to live with her friend Christine. Although it is a truism that people project their own desires on to texts, the difference in our two interpretations was so striking that I realized I had approached the search in a very specific way. My reaction to the letter initially had been emotional, and my immediate response – pragmatic, shallow and very speedy – was entirely consistent with my own character. I decided to read the letter yet again, trying as far as possible to strip out my preconceptions and prejudices. It was, of course, impossible, but perhaps the awareness was progress in itself.

'Forgive me for not having been able to find the words at that terrible moment when you slid through my fingers . . .'

Attempting to reread the letter with an open mind and a greater awareness of the palimpsest of possible interpretations, I was suddenly no longer certain that Maurice had drowned. I had been easily influenced by the watery imagery of the letter and had jumped to conclusions in a manner I now found breathtakingly foolish. Had I really visualized a boy in a tempestuous sea, his mother leaning far over the gunnels, her arms outstretched, their hands meeting through the foam, clasping, then being torn apart by the cruel seas as he 'slides from her fingers'? My preferred version had been less dramatic: a vicious teenage argument with an overprotective mother, in the aftermath of which Maurice had turned to the beach for solace, and taken his tiny sailing boat too far out to sea, or had simply swum too far out and been unable to make it back to the shore. In my imagination – and I had used my imagination for there was no mention of a boat, for instance – I had constructed this death, surrounded by water, sparked off by an argument ('Forgive me for being so angry . . .') caused by his impetuosity, his 'excess of desires'. It was natural to superimpose some version of the story on to the few available clues and, after all, others had jumped to the same conclusions. Or had I unconsciously projected my own interpretation without letting the other readers of the letter form their own opinions?

Had I simply watched too many films? Wasn't the letter-writer more likely to be a mother sitting by her sick child in hospital, seeing him slip slowly away from her? Perhaps his 'excess of desires' had led to a drug overdose, maybe as a result of a row? Or was it just that they had grown apart as he entered adolescence?

Now the letter seemed to me to be so unclear as to the cause of Maurice's death that I was horrified at my earlier certainty of judgement, based on so little evidence. Gathering statistics about the number of children drowned in France may have been a red herring. Trying to work out what happened to bodies lost at sea had been useless. I reassured myself that the time I had spent reading the regional press was not entirely lost, since I had anyhow concentrated more on the obituaries than on looking for articles about drowning.

I reviewed whether I could be bothered to continue searching. Had I been wasting my time not just looking for the wrong kind of death, but looking for the mother at all? Was it not time to give the bottle back to my friend the dog-walker or, with her permission, throw it back into the sea, or simply lock up the cupboard where it sat and get on with the rest of my own life? I was irritated with the ambiguity of the clues, but I still felt that I had many avenues to explore. If, at the end of doing so, my research had advanced no further, I would at least feel that I had tried.

I felt obliged to revisit the statistical information, and as quickly as possible. The lady at INED, the French government Institute of Demographic Studies, was at lunch when I rang back (and anyway I felt a little embarrassed at changing the cause of death after she had been so helpful). On reflection I felt that the Institute's data would be of limited use. The telephone number I had used for INSERM, the National Institute for Health and Medical Research, no longer responded. So, since I had to start from scratch, I tried to pretend to myself that this was a fresh lead. I would not explain to the bureau-crat why I was searching; I would just pretend to be a journalist researching childhood mortality – the death rates of boys aged, say, thirteen – in a very general way. Somehow this time I got straight through to the director.

He explained that at INSERM they looked at the death certifi-cates and classified the causes of death but then destroyed the documentation. This seemed very unlikely, and I pressed him on it, but he held to his story. My own story crumbled and I soon admitted that I was actually investigating one particular death, of one particular boy, whose name or date of death I did not know. After pointing out the utter hopelessness of my quest, the director told me that it was in fact INSEE, the National Institute for Statistics and Economic Studies, that held death records. However, I would need permission from CNIL, the National Commission for Computers and Freedom, to access anything. He wished me well.

While I was looking up the number for INSEE I was delighted to read on BT's website that, 'In France, the language is revered. Therefore when speaking it, do so with care. If your understanding of the language is poor, better to be safe and enquire after an English speaker.' Sound evidence in theory perhaps, but the next few numbers I rang resulted in a series of rapid answerphone messages, *en français naturellement*, referring me elsewhere, including freephone numbers that worked only from within France.

By the time I had discovered that this particular service of INSEE only supplied non-specific data for the European Union in its entirety, I felt I had spoken to enough French statisticians and bureaucrats to convince me that I had drained this particular well of information dry, shallow as it was.

When the lady in the Bibliothèque nationale had cast doubt on the psychological state of the letter-writer, and questioned that I should even attempt such a search without getting a psychiatric report, I had initially dismissed her. But if the letter-writer really was mad, should I not drop my search immediately?

I contacted a clinical psychologist at St Thomas's Hospital in London who reassured me. 'I see no evidence of mental illness,' she said after I had recounted my story, but then added, less helpfully, 'Unless of course she's made the whole thing up and there is no Maurice at all, in which case she's obviously completely mad.'

But she agreed that this was unlikely. 'Traditionally, in many societies, one year of mourning is seen as the time needed to recover from loss. In the case of the loss of a child, it is far longer. This woman seems to have no support from other people within her family, just the one friend. By writing this letter, sending this bottle, she is marking the end of her formal bereavement. And she is getting rid of a great deal of self-directed anger. Casting her story to the waves provides a form of rebirth for her.'

So not mad, or rather, not more mad than such a traumatic event would justify, just terribly sad.

I asked a friend who I knew had lost a son fifty years earlier – half a century before – how long it had taken her to be able to talk of his death. 'Until now,' she replied in a low voice. 'I have never spoken of it until now.' And then she told me how her three-year-old son had died and how life had not continued in any meaningful way for many years thereafter.

I also described the letter-writer's state of mind as well as I could to a general medical doctor. Having had my confidence in my analysis of Maurice's death so badly shaken by the realization that he may not have drowned, I now wanted as many people as possible with different areas of expertise to provide their opinions, just in case they picked up on some clue that had completely escaped me, or that I had wrongly interpreted.

To be fair, the doctor had very few actual symptoms on which to base his diagnosis. After I had assured him that in the circumstances I would settle for general impressions rather than a precise diagnosis, he agreed to share his opinion.

Perhaps trauma, he hazarded. A head injury, prolonged unconsciousness. A road accident, maybe. Soon he warmed up. A coma, perhaps, hence 'between two lights'. Unlikely to be cancer, since he left 'without warning' but probably not sudden, since he 'slipped away'.

Perhaps meningo-encephalitis. A meningococcal meningitis. There has been a lot of it around in recent years. That could lead to cerebral changes, coma. Maybe a cerebral tumour. Intake of ecstasy can cause cerebral effects. That would perhaps also tie in with her anger and over-indulgence of Maurice.

The doctor could rule nothing in or out, and I was no further forward.

The other pseudo-medical angle that I felt might shed some light on the state of mind of the missing mother was the viewpoint of a counsellor, someone who dealt with bereavement as an everyday occurrence and who certainly had more experience of it than I did. Perhaps the counsellor, with her trained perceptions, would be able to tell me how long ago the child had died, or to pick up on any other clues.

The counsellor was a psychoanalytic psychotherapist and had three children herself, two boys nearing Maurice's age. We had initially met through our sons, and while her professional view was clearly of most relevance, I thought the fact that she was also the mother of at least one son might provide her with some further insights.

'The first thing to emphasize,' she began, 'is that there are no certainties.'

Then, in a cliché of counselling, she asked me in a gentle tone of sympathy what I felt about the letter, about the letter-writer. I laughed. She smiled and continued her analysis.

'In a theoretical paradigm,' she began, 'of Freud through Lacan, it is a classic hysteric's letter – her first-born son is a substitute for her missing phallus (the phallus standing for differentiation – what is or isn't there). It seems there are no other children nor is there any mention of a father or reference to his absence. We can say that the paternal metaphor – *le nom/non du père* – which acts to protect the son from incest with the mother is not operative. You can feel how the son becomes a substitute for all her emotional and erotic needs – theoretically he becomes the phallus that the woman perceives herself as missing in the absence of her – the mother's – penis.'

I was already out of my depth with the terminology and very relieved when she veered away from Lacanian psychoanalysis to psychology on a more comprehensible level. 'In this way – and he is far from being alone – he will have felt smothered, buried alive by his mother's desire, expressed as devotion or aspiration. It is not perhaps surprising that around the time of puberty, when his own sexual life and desire might be stirring, there is some kind of rupture between them. It seems that an argument may have occurred which put pressure on mother and son. The closeness of the relationship may well have forced him into active rebellion in order to achieve some kind of separation from her.

'Unconsciously his choice was between remaining for ever in an alienated position, trying to fulfil what it was she wanted him to be, or to make an immense effort to escape – she was so symbiotically attached to him. It is not clear whether he really intended to hurt her in the only way he could, in other words by his escape. Given the nature of her attachment to her son, there is one sure way in which he could pay her out – and that is by harming himself.

'It seems there was an intense conflict with his mother when Maurice reached his teens but there are no clues as to the form this took, no references to the elements of the conflict. Yes, I do think, given all the watery language of the letter, it is probable that he drowned – or that there was some accident in the water, as a result of which he later died.

'The letter has an ornate, almost ritualistic quality. I get a picture of the mother as a Catholic woman, from a high-class French family, one of those families which takes its holidays on the coast. She used her son to fill the vacuum left by an unhappy marriage and an empty life. When she says that her life 'began with his birth', she hints at the revelation of having a first son; of being blessed at last with what has long been felt to be missing. A loss of this magnitude would take years to come to any kind of terms with. Yes, I would say more than five years. Given what he meant to her it is, in fact, amazing that she is still alive at all. I am pretty confident from the vocabulary and the detached tone of the writing that she has had some kind of help such as counselling.

'To have achieved the level of detachment that she strives for – although cannot maintain – the ability even to make this effort towards poetry, is impressive. It is written for an audience of herself. If she had not had some kind of therapy, the language would be more raw, and there would be more specific details – real clues about her identity and actual events – the things that happened. The literary language, the metaphorical style of the writing is her way of keeping her distance. It is as though she is always aiming for temperance.

'Now she has turned away from men and – it seems – towards a lesbian relationship. She lived in a world without a husband and father for her child and then she loses her son. With his loss, she loses the imaginary phallus that she temporarily acquired with his birth and it is as though she had to renounce the masculine in order to allow herself any kind of sexual life, a sexual life which until this point was sublimated in the love of her child.

'The mention of her friend Christine is a momentous step. This letter is a confessional to her son that allows her to make that move. He is the only one whose opinion she values. In her mind, she needs her son to be onside. The final sentence has a conversational tone that suggests he is still there, that she still needs to explain things directly to him. The unconscious reality expressed here is that he is still the one that matters. For her, he will always be the one. The real deal.'

The counsellor had provided me with a great deal of food for thought. I agreed that the absence of any mention of a father or partner in the letter was interesting and perhaps significant, though I could have done without the Lacanian interpretations. I thought she had put her finger on the suffocating nature of the relationship between mother and son, and managed to understand some of the intensity of that feeling. She had explained to me how the mother had managed to achieve a level of detachment from her grief by using beautiful imagery to push the experience further into the distance. And she had intellectualized what my gay friend had instinctively realized, that she was trying to replace the void left by Maurice's departure with a new lesbian relationship.

But apart from her suggestion that perhaps five years of counselling would have been required before the mother could achieve that level of emotional detachment, there were no concrete clues in her analysis, nothing to take me any closer to the writer of the letter.

10

Apart from my friend who had found the bottle, I knew three other people who lived in Kent: a doctor, a lawyer and a businessman who was a voluntary lifeboat man on the Isle of Sheppey. I decided to renew my friendship with the lifeboat volunteer.

From: Karen Liebreich
To: David
Subject: Letter in a bottle

Dear David,
Sorry to keep missing you. Are you still doing
voluntary shifts on the local lifeboat? I am very
interested in the tides on the beach at Warden Bay.

Do you remember, I mentioned a bottle we found
there? I need to find out where it might have come
from.

   I have spoken to my friend, who says the closest
she can work out about the tide that day is as
follows:

   It was Sunday 17 February 2002, late morning,
about 11 am that she found the bottle. It was up at
the high water mark.

   I know this isn't as precise as you would like,
but that's about as good as it gets.

Hope you are well.

Karen

Within a few weeks David had arranged a meeting with the local lifeboat skipper, so I rang my friend the dog-walker and she agreed to come with me. She had only read the letter once, when I sent her the rough translation. When I rang her and asked her opinion on various phrases she would never look at the letter in its entirety, so unwilling was she to torture her emotions by rereading it. But a day out at the lifeboat station was another matter.

The Isle of Sheppey is a place of marshes, dockyards, pubs and bitter self-mockery about inbreeding and strange island customs. Fifty miles from London, Sheppey lies at the mouth of the Thames, at its junction with the Medway, in north-east Kent. Separated from the mainland by the Swale, a tributary of the Thames, the island is some nine miles long and half as wide. Its north shore faces the North Sea.

As my friend and I approached Sheerness dockyard the flat light reflected from the windscreens of thousands of parked cars, laid out like jewels on a tray, awaiting transportation to dealers across the rest of the country. Most of Britain's imported cars enter the country via Sheerness. The security guards looked only mildly interested that we intended to visit the lifeboat station and raised the barrier with some bawdy comments.

A body in a dry suit was slumped over the handrail by the entrance to the boathouse. Was this a failed rescue attempt? Or was this how they hung up their equipment for speedy access in case of life or death? Later we were introduced to Dead Fred, an old suit now retained purely for decorative purposes. It certainly set the atmosphere.

Inside we met the cox, the only full-time, paid member of the team, who is apparently widely respected throughout the region for his knowledge of the local waters and tides. The rest of the team is made up of volunteers, reachable by pager.

The cox was a little gruff at first, living up to his sea-dog credentials. The slant of his eyebrows indicated that he thought our search was hopeless. However, he mellowed as we explained our quest and pulled out his charts and tide almanacs.

The high tides which could have deposited the bottle on a Sunday in February 2002 were as follows:

3 February 04.11

10 February 11.38

17 February 03.16

24 February 09.47

According to the cox, the bottle would have needed a north-easterly wind to bring it into Warden Bay. It could have been thrown from a boat, a yacht or a cross-Channel ferry, although he pointed out that there were few pleasure boats around that area in the winter months. He thought it might well have been thrown from an English beach – Norfolk was his preference – but since the Evian bottle had not been commercially available in the UK, I was doubtful of this. The cox pointed out that if you throw a bottle out on an incoming tide it might well just come straight back at you a few waves later, but it seemed to us very unlikely that a Frenchwoman would have brought a bottle available only on the continent to such a bleak, isolated beach in England with such inconvenient access. Thrown from a ferry, he thought it could have taken days or at most weeks to wash up.

99

Entering into the spirit of the search, he then checked the tides for the coast of northern France. Thrown from Brest, Cherbourg or the Breton ports, the bottle would have gone west towards America and Spain, taken the Gulf Stream down the Portuguese coast or spun in a never-ending circle somewhere off St Malo. From Dieppe eastwards, and from the Oostende region, it could have drifted towards the Isle of Sheppey.

We stared gloomily at his charts, trying to tease out an easy answer – or any answer – but in vain.

I believed what the lifeboat skipper had told me, but keen sailor friends suggested that I should double-check with the Royal Navy who had virtually invented tidal almanacs. So, just in case there was any loophole of information that the tidal patterns could supply, I also checked with the Hydrographic Office, part of the Ministry of Defence, who supply the information on which the tide tables are based. The man who answered my query informed me that for his training he had studied the tidal flow of oranges – good buoyancy, bright colour, not much wind resistance, eventually biodegradable – which could be used to predict tides to within a few minutes of accuracy. But his email reply suggested that the bottle's launching point was not so easy to track backwards:

    Unfortunately it is practically impossible to say
    where and when the bottle entered the sea. In
    addition to pure tidal streams, there will also have
    been weather effects (i.e. wind) acting upon the
    bottle at any given time which may have resulted in
    it moving in an unpredictable way.

So the tides retained their secret. The bottle could still have come from almost anywhere along the northern French or Belgian coast, or been thrown from a boat.

When I was trying to find out more about the history of letters in bottles, and objects drifting around the seas, one name kept cropping up. I had first heard about Curtis Ebbesmeyer, a Seattle-based oceanographer, when a flush of rubber ducks began to wash up around the world's beaches, attracting media interest. In January 1992 a North Pacific storm dislodged 29,000 bath toys from their container on an ocean-going freighter – and the Rubber Duck Flotilla was launched. Since 1966 Dr Ebbesmeyer has been mapping sea currents. At first he used to drop buoys and markers and follow their progress, but then he realized he could use existing shipping debris. Now Ebbesmeyer is 'the big Kahuna' of beachcombers. He tracks the cargo that manages to make its escape from the 100 million or so containers that are shipped around the world each year. Apparently, 10,000 of these containers – each 8 by 40ft, containing, say, 10,000 trainers – fall overboard and their contents are dispersed across the seven seas. Ebbesmeyer's calculations are surprisingly sophisticated. He factors in wind resistance: shoes, for example, tend to float upside down, offering zero wind profile, while rubber ducks' heads catch the breeze. So a duck takes about three years to go round the North Pacific, whereas a trainer takes six. In the millennium year 2000 a million pieces of Lego were lost from three containers in the Atlantic and are expected to make their way to land via the Arctic and the North-East Passage. Ebbesmeyer expects some of them to arrive on Alaskan beaches in 2012 and on Washington beaches in 2020.

Apparently he has never found a letter in a bottle.

Beaches have their own specialities and, in an article for *National Geographic*, Ebbesmeyer explained, 'They're like restaurants – some serve Thai food, some Indian or Chinese food. Some beaches are known for their glass or driftwood or artefacts.' Some serve sea beans, seeds that have fallen from trees and plants that grow on shores around the world, mainly in tropical climes, and there is a whole sea bean subculture that collects them, identifies them, polishes them and writes about them.

Dr Ebbesmeyer runs Beachcombers' Alert, 'a place on the web where beachcombers from around the world obtain and exchange information'. I decided to ask his advice about the bottle. I sent him all the details I had about where the letter had been found. He answered my email with unnerving swiftness a few seconds later:

```
Dear Karen,
Thanks for providing as much information as you can.
I'm afraid there are just not enough details to
go on.
Please let me know further progress,
Curt
```

Before talking to the artist's three contacts, I wanted to resolve for myself, once and for all, the issue of births, deaths and marriages. When I first thought of looking for the unknown mother, I had reviewed various strategies, but the most likely to be successful had always seemed to me to be either the local papers or the registry of deaths. I had had confidence in old-fashioned archival leg-work, using the local press or the death registry.

At the beginning of my search I had been put off by what the international undertakers who worked with the Foreign Office had told me about the lack of a centralized register of deaths in France, but given the key role this could play in resolving the mystery, I had to be sure. I could find no sign of a French register on the internet. I contacted the British version and they put me through to the department specializing in overseas registers. The lady confirmed that the French have no such register, and that all records are held in the local town halls. I asked if, in the UK, it would be possible to track down someone with only a first name and an age, with no date or location of death. No, I was told, of course not.

Back in France once more, I picked a town hall. Since the odds of finding the one *mairie* that held Maurice's details were so unfavourable, it seemed to make little difference where I started. The capital was most congenial and convenient for me, and presumably held the largest registry, so I decided to start with the closest. The births, deaths and marriages register had been so important to my search that I felt I still could not take at face value the information about the regional system but needed to go to a local archive and see if a personal appearance could charm – or persuade, or nag, or even bribe – someone into unlocking a magical database somewhere. I found it hard to credit that a modern nation famously unified by Napoleon, a nation where legend claimed that the Minister for Education knew exactly what each French child was doing at a specific time of day throughout the country, would not have a centralized archive of its population details.

The *mairie* of the 16th arrondissement was ostentatiously massive.

Bedding plants flanked an entrance that asserted its nineteenth-century civic pomposity. An ornate staircase led upwards to corridors in which harassed citizens hurried past clutching sheaves of documents. At one doorway a woman implored an official, 'There must be a solution.' She pleaded and wept as the bureaucrat gently closed the door in her face.

An 'administrative agent' had agreed to see me and talk me through the system. She was an older woman with streaky blonde hair, heavily made up and manicured, and with a wrinkled décolleté emphasized by a skimpy cardigan. At first she was delighted to show off her knowledge, limited as it was. Yes, the records were kept there for one hundred years. Then they were sent off to a national archive in some boulevard in the 19th arrondissement. From 1989 onwards, records were held on computer in the local town hall, with a duplicate record of death being sent to the town hall where the person had been born. She twisted the computer screen slightly so that I could see the columns of deaths, and indeed I soon spotted a Maurice, deceased in December 1996.

The picture was even more fragmented than I could have guessed. Not only does each part of Paris have its own *mairie* – so there is one for the 17th arrondissement, one for the 11th – and therefore its own register, but you also need individual official permissions from the Procureur Général to access the data. There were twenty town halls in

Paris alone, requiring twenty such requests for permission and twenty individual searches for a partial entry that was statistically unlikely to be in that town hall. So the undertaker had told the truth about the 36,000 local *mairies* throughout France. The dead end was genuine.

Perhaps the administrative agent had seen my eyes light up at the sight of the dead Maurice; at any rate she suddenly took fright and spun the screen abruptly away from me, muttering that I must first produce the personal authorization from the Procureur Général that could be acquired at the Tribunal de Grande Instance. It would also apparently cover a few other town halls under that particular Pooh-Bah's jurisdiction. She leaned forward and reached for my notes, scratching her name and phone number on my pad with such force that she damaged several sheets below. 'You mustn't use it,' she whispered. I reassured her, but she had lost confidence and shooed me vigorously away from her desk.

The meeting had reached its conclusion. It seemed true beyond a shadow of doubt that the register of births, deaths and marriages was only accessible via the individual town halls and with special individual authorization.

11

My two best hands were played out, but I still had a few cards up my sleeve. I had not fully utilized the miracle of internet technology, and I had not yet been in touch with the New Age contacts supplied by the artist on her little orange notelet. I would save the alternative therapies for later, and try the high-tech solutions first.

After the failure of the corporate databases to resolve the issue early on in my search, I had occasionally spent idle moments rifling through search engines for Boolean combinations of 'Maurice + noyé + treize' ('Maurice + drowned + thirteen') but since my realizing that his death was not necessarily the result of drowning I had not dedicated an adequate amount of time to the matter. Now I set aside time to search all possible permutations and combinations.

I typed in 'Maurice + mort' and was rewarded by an article about a recently published children's book entitled *Maurice est mort*. The reviewer liked it – she thought it helped children to see that there is nothing terrifying about death, and that the dead would be released from the trivia of everyday irritations. I ordered it, pleased by the coincidence of the name and wondering whether it had any relevance to my search. Perhaps the author had known Maurice?

It was horrid. Two little birds are playing and one shoots the other by mistake. The dead one, Maurice, is superficially inspected by a doctor who cannot stop thinking about his dinner, shown in bubbles above his head. Then the dead bird is nailed into a coffin and eaten by worms. The unpleasant coincidence of the dead bird's name merely emphasized once again the horrible finality of Maurice's fate. Thinking about a caricature bird nailed up in a little brightly coloured coffin instead of a dead child was no consolation.

I tried to deploy the technological breadth of the internet as best I knew. I set up a small website with a plea for information, and linked it with several larger, busier sites. I wrote an email appeal containing the few facts that I possessed and bulk emailed it to all my friends and acquaintances, asking them to send it on to all their friends and acquaintances. The message snowballed out from my computer in a real-time effort to test the theory that everyone in the world was now only six degrees of separation away from everyone else. One of my friends replied that he was sending it on immediately to his address book of 5,500 people. At low moments in my search, I would console myself that my message was being forwarded through cyberspace and would eventually end up on the screen of someone who had known Maurice or his mother.

A few weeks later I received an email from an American academic querying whether the whole thing was a mathematical hoax.

```
What is given are ages (13), standard rebus clues —
decede, deceased — which is DCD, 900 in bad Latin
numerals, and names: Maurice and Christine (which
makes me think of Christine de Pizan, or Christine
de Suède, or Maurice de Saxe). The rest of the main
message is a triple oxymoron, reminiscent of surreal-
ist poetry: you can't 'extinguish rest', 'rest' can't
be 'tireless', and 'outstretched arms' aren't at
'rest'. So seeing as there's nothing else to speak
of, the whole thing looks like a puzzle or a test or
a brainteaser to me. It is not a moving message, it
is a totally implausible piece of French put together
from probable allusions, quotations and fixed phrases.
I haven't cracked the code. But I will eat my hat if
this is not part of a plot of some kind.
```

All this seemed unconvincing to me – I thought 900 would be CM in Latin numerals; I didn't see what a fourteenth-century poet, an eighteenth-century general and a seventeenth-century Catholic convert would have in common – and if we were looking for name associations, why not Maurice Chevalier and Christina Aguilera? However, I was open to any possible source of help so I immediately contacted the American and asked whether I could send him the whole message. He agreed and, once he had studied the complete letter, wrote to retract his original analysis. 'Sorry for my previous suspicions – this is no coded prank.' His new analysis agreed with mine, which was reassuring but also a pity, since the rebusian triple oxymoron had held out the promise of an interesting intellectual challenge.

Meanwhile I redoubled my internet efforts. I found the French equivalent of Friends Reunited, *Les amis sont réunis*, and asked them to put out an appeal. The automatic response asked me for my school and years of attendance.

I trawled the net for sites referring to letters in bottles, and was amazed at the differences between them, differences that seemed to epitomize the disparity in international cultures. The British site, www.letterinabottle.com, was very down-to-earth.

Letter in a Bottle is pleased to offer a gift that is original and of the highest quality. We use only the best materials to ensure a finished product that will surprise and delight. This memorable message in a bottle gift can be used to convey a message that will never be forgotten, always remembered and valued.

Each Letter in a Bottle is hand assembled and finished to the highest standards with meticulous attention to detail. This ensures that each bottle and its letter and message has been assembled with loving care, using only the finest imported bottles and after applying our original designs and finishing touches. Letter in a Bottle is a British-based craft business.

I sent a request for help – perhaps the website could include a small advert about my search – but received no reply.

The Californian version, www.messageinabottle.com, spoke less of craft and more of the sea air . . .

Is it our proximity to the ocean that fires our designers' imagination in creating our magnificent bottles? Is it the stimulus they receive from contemplating breathtaking seascapes that serves in their creative process? Or is it the natural beauty from the rolling hills to the windswept cypress trees to the quaint shops that do this? We believe it is all of these.

This idyllic setting, where the salt air is permeated with romance and good times, is one of our greatest assets in creating bottles that are able to inspire poems and love letters alike. It is our hope that our bottles will inspire you.

III

Within a day I had a courteous reply offering to help, and imme-diately sent off information and a photograph of the bottle. This was posted on the website shortly afterwards but attracted no response.

The English and American sites were purely consumer-orientated, though from a poetic and artisanal point of view naturally, while the French site was mournful and cathartic.

'Bouteille à la mer', www.unebouteillealamer.com, showed a sad little bottle floating on the screen, surrounded by tears.

Fed up of living, of solitude, anguish, depression? Write down your words, put them in a bottle, then throw them into the internet ocean . . . The bottle will break, and somewhere someone will read your words.

. . . The author of this site is qualified in clinical and pathological psychol-ogy. He has worked for the last ten years in a psychiatric hospital and spends the greater part of his time carrying out psychological follow-ups to patients in a clinic attached to this hospital . . . The theoretical application on which his practical work is based derives from Jacques Lacan.

The aim of this site is not to provide a specific response to suffering. It serves merely as a springboard to suffering, that it may travel and touch someone by the randomness of its voyage. The person who receives the message may choose whether to reply or not, but whatever the choice, the message will have been read.

Permitting oneself to throw the mask of grief into the water and address the unknown is perhaps the first step towards seeing a smile in one's reflection.

When I contacted the webmaster, who was indeed a practising clinical psychologist, he explained that he had launched the site a few years earlier, in June 2002. In its first year it had received some 8,500 visits. 'What counts,' he wrote to me, 'is the hope that one's internal suffering may be heard, sooner or later, just as when one seals a letter into a bottle. The hope of a reply counts for more than the reply itself.'

Some people, especially adolescents, seem to become addicted to the site itself, and visit it when they are feeling depressed and experience the need to confide their secrets to a stranger. When the webmaster receives an SOS he passes it on to someone who has signed up as being willing to receive messages. He himself only replies if the messages request information about psychology or psychotherapy.

Each site – American, British, French – seemed to represent clichéd views of its country of origin: the British small-scale and hand-crafted, the American with its face to the ocean waves and its initial customer-friendliness, and the French site intellectual and inward-looking.

The French webmaster was intrigued by my quest and also offered to help. The thought crossed my mind that perhaps he saw me as a patient in need of psychiatric attention. His email read:

```
You could send me a copy of the message your friend
found. It is possible that the author has also left
a similar message on the 'letter in a bottle' site.
With a copy, I could compare the message with those
on the site, and see if the same person has indeed
left a message. Also, as I live in the north of
France (Lille), I could try to contact people and
organizations who deal with those who have lost a
dear one. I think there is a strong possibility that
the author of the SOS sent it from a beach in north-
ern France or Belgium.

    Chance and fate are sometimes troubling, so
perhaps it would be possible to find this person.
```

I sent him several paragraphs from the letter and encouraged him to do what he could to further the search.

As he became more involved, he set up a page about the letter on his website, and cross-referenced it to a few other French sites with which he had contacts, including a French *chansonnier*. The request for help sat curiously amongst the discography of the pop star.

The quest began to preoccupy the French psychologist even when he went on holiday. On his return he wrote to me, 'I think that the person lives somewhere near Calais or Boulogne. There is a place, Cap

Gris Nez, whose scenery lends itself perfectly to the idea of throwing in a letter in a bottle. When I saw the place, I just had this feeling, this intuition.' Cap Gris Nez is a headland with spectacular views over the White Cliffs of Dover, situated on the D940 between Calais and Boulogne. He had no proof other than his intuition, but he decided to throw some of his own professional resources at the problem, and I was delighted to encourage him.

He set one of his researchers to contact all the town halls situated along the coast. He also asked his father-in-law, a policeman in the region, to check out any police databases that might contain records of Maurice's death. At a conference on bereavement and offering support to parents who have lost children, one of his colleagues, based in Cherbourg, spoke about the letter in the bottle and appealed to the delegates for information on the letter-writer. Thus the information was passed on to similar associations in France, and the psychologist assured me that it would only be a matter of time before we received some concrete information about the identity of Maurice and his mother.

As yet, I have had no positive response from any of these encouraging attempts, although the psychologist/webmaster remains in contact, and sends me periodical updates on the lack of progress from his efforts.

Meanwhile, the excitement of the chase had gripped me, eclipsing the sorrow that lay at the heart of my quest. I hadn't even read the letter for a while and its raw emotions had faded into the background.

I was now hunting for a quarry.

When I spoke to friends and acquaintances about what I was doing, it turned out that many of them had found mysterious messages, poignant snapshots of other people's lives. A painter acquaintance, for instance, had discovered a love poem tucked down the side panel of his second-hand Mercedes the week before. He had no idea whether it had ever been delivered but the message was permeated with despair at the fading beauty of the woman and the relationship. It was folded neatly and inserted so far down the side that it could not have got there by accident. Only a few days before, my brother had found a strangely analytical love letter written on the back of a pub menu in Salamanca:

- Do you know what you want from life?
- Do you know how to get it?
- Am I part of the life you want?
- Are you prepared to make an effort to be together?
- Do you think it's worth the bother?
- The most important thing is that I love you, and I have

already asked myself these questions and the answer is yes.
But I can't be half-and-half, Jorge, I have to give 100% or
I can't give at all.

So the desire to track *objets trouvés* back to their authors was not a private obsession. I discovered a website, www.foundmagazine.com, devoted solely to the scraps of paper, photos, even audio tapes that people had found floating around on the street, or in car parks, fragments of other people's lives.

We collect love letters, birthday cards, kids' homework, to-do lists, ticket stubs, poetry on napkins, doodles – anything that gives a glimpse into someone else's life. Anything goes . . . we wanted to make a magazine so that everyone can check out all the strange, hilarious and heartbreaking things people have picked up.

But nowhere on the website did I find a letter in a bottle like the one washed ashore on the Isle of Sheppey.

The only real, incontrovertible fact that I knew about the writer's background was that she had watched the film *Message in a Bottle*. I began to wonder if she had copied other sections of the letter, perhaps from more literary sources unknown to me. I had been thinking about where to turn next for advice when the morning post brought the latest copy of my college alumni magazine.

I had been struggling for some hours with *Lacan for Beginners*, so the magazine seemed to offer light relief by comparison. The first article was a profile of the new Master, a renowned professor of French literature and, by a miracle of coincidence, an expert on Lacan. It seemed to me to be a propitious sign. A professor of French literature with a sideline in Lacanian psychotherapy – what more could I ask? My request for a meeting met with success. The Professor was intrigued.

12

The great wooden doors of the college were just as I recalled them. Ancient, heavy, impressive, designed to bar the hoi-polloi from the tranquil groves of Academe. Beyond lay the perfect O of the lawn and, in the far corner of First Court, the entrance to the Master's Residence. During my time at Cambridge I had followed my own path and had never been invited to cross its portals. The twenty years since I had last been in that courtyard represented just a short breath in the history of the college but a large chunk of my own life. Now I hesitated outside the building, looking up at the college motto, founder Margaret Beaufort's *Souvent me souvient* – I often remember. How uncannily appropriate in both language and content. I had no recollection of noticing it before.

The Professor was in his early sixties, his grey hair just skimming

his collar, his manner welcoming as he came to greet me at the entrance of his lodge. His graciousness suited the antiquity and opulence of the establishment, with its Canalettos casually lining the walls. Before climbing the stairs to his drawing room, the Professor selected a book from an enormous set of shelves that filled a corridor leading to a further wing of the residence. I glanced at the title as we went upstairs. It was a book of verse by Rimbaud.

We settled into deep armchairs and the Professor began to speak, fluently and with a sensitivity and perception that impressed me, and made me wish I could talk and think with such coherence and eloquence. I had sent him a copy of the letter the previous week in the hope that he would find the time to prepare himself for our meeting.

'We have to face the possibility,' he began, 'that this could be a work of fiction and that the writer is consciously or unconsciously immersing herself in a very active and vigorous French literary tradition in putting this text together. It is either a real message or an elaborate hoax, using various literary devices and the classic one of a message in a bottle, in order to titillate the finder, without providing an account of the actual family circumstances or emotions that are described.'

'So do you not think it is real?' I asked bluntly. The thought that it was a hoax had of course crossed my mind. The possibility that it might be a literary joke had not.

'It has a feeling of reality about it,' he conceded. 'It seems to me to read like a report on experience and on personal feelings, yet at the same time one has to remind oneself that literary texts themselves often have that quality – of personal disclosure, reportage sharing intimate thoughts, secrets, with the reader. I would question whether this might be a solitary, strange, rather desolate act of publication, throwing the text into the sea in a bottle . . . hoping for one reader. It could be the first step towards publication of a very elaborate piece of literary artifice, although I'd much rather think of it as a statement from a bereaved mother about her own pain and her own loss. I'd like to think there was a real family and a real human situation in the background, rather than yet another work of literature.'

I was doubtful and questioned whether such an inefficient method of publication would be considered by someone merely writing the letter as a literary artifice or a hoax.

'There's an element in the whole thing which is not straightforward confessional, not a simple cry for help, but is mediated through a mass of received literary images, texts. That's the element that seems to suggest that something else is going on, something more than a mere expression of personal feeling and loss.' The Professor fumbled for his copy of the letter. 'I want to read you a fragment or two that struck me as ingenious beyond the needs of the occasion, passages that suggest that a spontaneous striving for literary effect is overriding simple questions of self-expression.' He found the phrase in the letter and read it out: '"Sans prévenir il s'est derobé à la vie dans un trop plein de désirs, un trop vif de vivance, à l'aurore de l'été."' ('Without warning, he slipped away from life in an excess of desires, too full of vivid life, at the dawn of summer.')

'The "trop plein de désir" is itself a rather elaborate phrase, trying to convey this thirteen-year-old's appetite for life, his vitality, his energy, the multiplicity of his wishes, plans, projects and so forth. It's already "un trop plein" – an overflow system, within the world of plumbing, hydraulics and so forth – it is quite a refined phrase with a lot going on in it. The next phrase, however, "un trop vif de vivance", plays on the writer's own rather unusual use of the word "vivance" earlier in the letter; it's not an overflow, it's an over-life of vitality that's being spoken about, and "vivance" has a semi-technical sense to it. This suggests to me that the writer is half in love with her own literary language, and with her own ingenuity, as well as keeping a motherly eye on the lost child at the beginning, at the dawn, of his summer flowering, "à l'aurore de l'été". And this is a haunting phrase. Since first reading this letter, I have thought to myself how extraordinary that the French language, handled by an ordinary person – and she sounds ordinary in other respects – should be able to achieve this degree of intensity as the letter unfolds.' He hesitated for a moment, and I suspect we were both thinking of the unknown ordinary person who had touched our emotions.

The Professor continued his analysis. 'There is also the language of the weather, of seascapes, of the movement of waves, of winds, that is to say the whole natural world caught up in the life and the life expectancy of the individual, and the desolation of the bereaved person. This is something that nineteenth-century French poetry often does, and very movingly, too. One thinks of Victor Hugo, for example, as perhaps the supreme exponent of this orchestration to harmonize the movements of nature with the movements of human subjectivity. To find an ordinary person doing the same thing with such skill and such élan really is impressive. For me, as a literary scholar, it is that much more moving to find literary language being used in this way, as if it were part of everyone's patrimony, whatever questions one may ask about authenticity. So this is not just a moving personal document, it talks about the uses of literature in ordinary life in a way that is itself cogent and compelling.'

I had never thought of language in that way before and somehow his words seemed to push open an unused door for me. Through the crack I could perceive a whole new landscape of thought that I had never even known was there.

Meanwhile, the Professor was thumbing through the book he had brought upstairs with him. 'One of the strangest of Rimbaud's prose poems in his collection *Illuminations*, entitled 'Dévotion', uses this particular formula, which is that of a toast, raising a glass to someone.' He read out part of the poem:

'*A l'adolescent que je fus. A ce saint vieillard, ermitage ou mission. A l'esprit des pauvres . . .*'

'To the youth I once was. To this holy old man, hermitage or
mission.
To the spirit of the poor . . .

'I had long had a soft spot for Rimbaud. Many years ago on the Karakorum Pass between China and Pakistan, one of the highest roads in the world, I had met a man whose father was a CIA operative. I was taking the bus, he was cycling, and we were staying in an overnight hostelry. We became friends and over the years he would write to me from various hotspots in the world – Iran, Iraq, Afghanistan, Chile. Coups and shattering events would follow wherever he cycled and I developed a theory that he had followed his father's profession and his cycling holidays were not entirely innocent. During his travels he carried a book of Rimbaud's poetry and, on the rare occasions when he did return, home was a boat called *Rimbaud* moored on the Pacific. There would always be a moment of tension as he approached the dock after an absence of months or years, the suspense of whether the boat would still be afloat, although with the advent of email he hoped someone would inform him if she ever actually sank. My friend would don a mask and swim under the keel to inspect the hull. Then he would work at varnishing other people's boats for a few weeks and earn enough for a few links of chain or some caulking materials or whatever he most needed for his dilapidated home. Having done the bare minimum to keep her afloat, he would take off again on his bicycle around the world. As far as I knew, *Rimbaud* never sailed anywhere, and my friend is cycling still, but at the time the romance of his life and his reading matter had encouraged me to investigate the poet.

'The formula is used with great ingenuity in this poem by Rimbaud,' the Professor continued. '"Dévotion", as an act of paying tribute, and also as a semantic, lexical exploration of the possible meanings of the preposition "à". Now something similar is going on in the opening of this letter; that is to say the writer is simply listing the intended recipients, "A tous les navires . . ." ["To all ships . . ."] but she is doing it in a way that brings disparate strands together, so that there's a sense of them being threaded up, of different things being brought together in a new pattern, and this straightforward syntactic pattern is being complicated – complexified, one might say – as these phrases unfold. So that from the very beginning we are presented with something that reads like literature as distinct from something that reads like a simple confessional.'

I told him that although I thought the mother started by addressing us all, it gradually became clear that the letter was really only addressed to her son. The Professor agreed that naming the son, Maurice, was a dramatic moment. 'But then she comes round to talking about her friend, so the friend becomes the co-addressee, and in the very last flourish of the letter the friend is named. So between Maurice, the son, and Christine, the fellow addressee, a little triangular drama begins to emerge. There are certain things one can only say to one's son when mediated through the presence of a third party.'

The Professor suggested that perhaps the friend had emboldened the letter-writer to put her feelings into words, and possibly had even suggested putting the letter in a bottle and throwing it into the sea as an act of exorcism, or catharsis. On the one hand, he thought that bringing in a third person at the end of the letter added an unmistakably personal touch. On the other hand, he wondered 'whether that very act of triangulation of the three persons is not the superimposition of a certain sort of literary form – a really rather elaborate literary construction – upon what might otherwise be a rather shapeless mass of personal impressions.'

I said I thought it strange that, if it *was* a literary artifice, it should be confined to the very last lines of the letter and the Professor agreed, though with some complex phrasing: 'The placing of it at the end would incline me to think of the thing as backing up the authenticity theory rather than the put-up theory.'

At this point I tentatively brought up the subject of psychoanalysis, although dreading that I might be opening another floodgate of incomprehensible Lacanian jargon. The Professor eagerly seized on the suggestion, seeing the introduction of Christine as a way of facilitating the dialogue and unblocking the relationship between the other two characters in the story. 'So that Christine, whether or not the author has a personal relationship with her, is acting as a gate-keeper or as an empowerer, moving the whole of the narrative into a new phase.'

I breathed a sigh of relief. That had all been fairly clear and comprehensible. He had not even mentioned Lacan.

Although the Professor had already touched on the subject of the writer's literary influences, I pressed him harder. Could he tell from the letter what kind of books she had read? I asked. He had clearly been considering the question. 'My guess is that she has read a lot of nineteenth-century poetry by Hugo, Rimbaud, Baudelaire, possibly by Lamartine, and that she is well-read in the prose literature of the same period, often called poetic prose or prose poems. Those are two separate genres or sub-genres but tend to produce the same sort of writing: the interrelationship between human feeling and the move-ments of nature, and the combining of both – nature and feeling – within the syntax. Examples of that can be found all over the place in nineteenth-century French literary writing.'

I asked if he could see any direct plagiarization from other works. 'No,' he shook his head sadly. 'It's a matter of regret to me that I can't, because I cannot help feeling that as a professional in the field of French literature I should have been able to track down various things. But what I do take from the letter is a general sense of the writer's immersion in nineteenth-century French poetry and poetic prose. That is a language of exaltation and uplift, a language of emotional intensity, which in itself shelves away into another language that I know much less about, the language of religious consolation. My guess is that there are a number of tracts and pamphlets that talk about loss, pain, bereavement and consolation, and the importance of an afterlife, whether of a celestial or terrestrial kind. There are moments, whether of personal originality or just of a more cunning, more resourceful borrowing from other sources, where the language becomes markedly more intense. It leaves the popular prayer-book literature far behind, and evolves into something richer and stranger, a literature of supercharged expressiveness. I'd like to think, of course – one is always on the lookout for unacknowledged geniuses – that here is an ordinary person who has suddenly risen to new heights of expression and become a writer in her own right and for her own end.' He paused, then shrugged. 'But it could be that, if there is borrowing going on that this is just a more artful form of borrowing.'

Since the Professor had mentioned the literature of religious consolation, I asked him what he thought about the elements of New Age spirituality in the letter.

'She's got this from a whole international literature of New Age writing, much of it in French, much translated from Anglo-American into French. What causes me to hesitate somewhat about that as a major element in explaining this text is that New Ageism as I understand it tends to indulge in fantasy solutions of one kind or another; it tends to envelop things in spiritual happy-talk. But what *this* writer is doing instead is reintroducing the heavy tread of mortality into the sentences: "I had you, you were mine, you were close to me and you've gone, and there's nothing I can do about it. And my writing in one sense can just keep on retelling the story of your loss, of your being lost." So there's something down-to-earth and dour and minimalist about the writing as well. This is what it feels like to be a bereaved mother, this is the inescapable absence that my life is permeated by. And that runs counter to the New Age optimism and rosy-huedness in very interesting ways.'

The Professor had put his finger on the essential bleakness of the letter, the inexorable fact of Maurice's death.

Did he think she was a professional writer? 'I would say not. She is somebody who has written before, and read a lot. Possibly she's a teacher, used to helping others with their writing, used to writing personal letters to friends and family. She prides herself on her literary craft. But she is not somebody who works at this for a career. There are no real indications of professionalism; the handwriting, the punctuation, occasionally the spelling suggests a sort of spontaneous overflow of literary language directed towards the expression of personal feelings.'

I then told the Professor about the film from which the writer had drawn some paragraphs. I had first let him dig a hole for himself with his literary analysis, but he had avoided the trap. He expressed his relief at not having made any erroneous deductions about the literary sources of those particular lines from *Message in a Bottle*, and without missing a beat he absorbed the information into his analysis. 'Of course knowing that there's a Hollywood movie in the background causes one to ask all sorts of further questions about authenticity or otherwise. Now, it could be that the film produced a sudden sense of empowerment, suggested an available format for saying something that was highly personal. So it could give one the licence to make statements that otherwise would be impossible. Or could it be that the message-in-a-bottle formula, being a cliché, is just a part of the general ebb and flow of human communication that doesn't mean anything in particular? It's the clichédness of the message-in-a-bottle formula that I would question. These are forms that have the power to imprint themselves on our imagination.'

I wasn't sure I could cope with the direction of this line of thought, so I drew the Professor's attention to the handwriting, but he shrugged it off, saying that to him it looked just like that of an average French schoolgirl. He was concerned to give me a warning: 'One needs to exercise a sort of methodological suspicion when faced with documents of this kind if one is doing the forensic task that you seem to have set yourself, that is to say understanding the emotional world that this writer inhabits. If one is going to undertake such a task, one needs to ask oneself, "Is what I see really there? Is what I think is happening in the here-and-now really happening in the more remote past?" You must be wary of false leads, and attaching straightforward solutions to the problem. I'm saying nothing more than what Hercule Poirot would say to the local vicar.'

By now I was a little lost. How would you go about finding the writer, I queried, but the Professor turned the question on its head and began to analyse my motivation. 'I think your wish to find her is interesting in itself. Finding any anonymous manuscripts, whether from a period when these were common, as in the Middle Ages in France, or from the modern world, tends to set one off on a quest for an author. If I find a sheet of orchestral music without a signature, without clues to help identify the composer, I want to know by internal or external evidence whether this is Schubert or Beethoven or Mozart . . . and that wish itself is quite interesting and worth speculating about. Another way of approaching the question would be to say that the world is full of texts, of disclosures, confessions of feeling. As one travels on the London Underground, one overhears fragments of other people's conversations and one is momentarily drawn into other people's lives. Take mobile phone conversations, for instance. It would be odd in cases like that to want to identify the speakers, to track them down, to give them a biography, a personal place in history. It would be a better approach to such material to let it all happen, to let it wash over one, as part of the ebb and flow of meaning in the human world.'

I was captivated by this view of waves of text and meaning splashing over me wherever I went, and the vision of myself being gradually driven into an asylum by the attempt to identify the source of each sliver of overheard conversation.

'But you don't want this letter to be part of the ebb and flow of meaning in the human world. You want it to have an author,' the Professor continued. And you want to be able to see this person. Perhaps meet her and ask what really happened – Have you recovered from your bereavement, and so forth. It's not that I'm suspicious of that wish, because it's a wish I've had myself, finding ancient correspondence. But wanting to have it all buttoned down, and identified, and docketed, and placed in some sort of museum of significant texts, is only one way of approaching communicative acts of this kind. Another way would be to regard this as a valuable human document in its own terms, whether or not the writer is still alive, and leave it at that. Instead, you're setting off on a kind of quest, a Grail quest, for an author and a concrete personal situation behind the text. And that's a labour-intensive way of going about things. I don't envy you the task.'

Perhaps I should take the Professor's advice and file the letter away in my memory, putting the time I had already spent searching for the writer into a box of experience that had taught me something about myself and improved my French vocabulary. But each time I considered giving up, I thought I would make just one more effort – one more email, one more phone call, one more visit to the library. The answer might be round the next corner.

The teacher in him reasserted itself and the Professor drew my attention to developments in French literature today. 'Ordinary lives, ordinary factual reports on average people doing average things have come to enjoy a whole new prestige. During the '60s and '70s, texts were so obsessed with their own internal workings and their relationships with earlier and contemporary writing that their human content was either drained away or became largely inaccessible through the shadow-play of literary self-consciousness. But in the '90s the idea grew that literature shouldn't aim for a grand generality in human affairs, but for closely observed detail. There's something in this writing that suggests the writer is aware of that.'

We had ground to a halt and I was no nearer discovering the letter-writer's identity. As the Professor showed me to the door I asked him whether he had found the letter moving.

'I *was* moved by it,' he replied in a slight tone of surprise. 'I wasn't particularly expecting to be. I suppose I was rather suspicious of the message-in-a-bottle formula, thinking it very, very improbable that anything of note should emerge on the seashore, washed up on the Channel coast. But I found the inventiveness of the writing, its rhythm and straightforwardness, the sense of a very simple personal tale being unfolded paragraph by paragraph, haunting. And I too wanted to know more about this person and how Maurice came to be lost, how the mourning came to be instigated. And how writing of this kind came to be thought an appropriate response to that personal tragedy. So my curiosity was tickled by the whole thing. But more than that, my human sympathies. And I showed the letter to my wife and she had the same sort of response.' He paused for a moment. 'In fact it moved her to tears straight away.'

As I walked across First Court, the chapel bells rang out over centuries of college tranquillity, and I thought about the strange journey of the letter which, from a desolate beach in Kent, had made the wife of a professor in Cambridge weep.

13

'Who *is* my reader? . . . Every book is a message in a bottle tossed into the sea with the hope it will reach a different shore. I feel very grateful when someone finds it and reads it, particularly someone like Noriega.'

> Isabel Allende, *My Invented Country*, on hearing that
> General Noriega had been arrested with two books:
> the Bible and her novel *The House of the Spirits*

The Professor had said that the letter-writer was imbued with the spirit of Hugo, Rimbaud and other nineteenth-century authors. I realized that my lack of knowledge of French literature was so complete that I had not even seen the musical *Les Misérables*. There was a cultural abyss to fill. In my ignorance, Victor Hugo seemed the most accessible.

I started with *Les Misérables*. There were phrases that jumped out at me – in so far as anything can jump from a book over a thousand pages long. A man who has slipped overboard swims on for hours in a desperate struggle for life. 'He feels at once buried by these two infinities, the sea and the sky; one is a tomb, the other a shroud.' The letter-writer had used the imagery of sky and sea, but for her the sky was an escape rather than a shroud. It was not much to show for the many pages consumed.

Three years after *Les Misérables*, Hugo wrote a fragment called *The Sea and the Wind* that was initially supposed to have formed part of *Toilers of the Sea*. In it he wrote: 'One can hear the sob of creation. The sea is the great mourner. She takes on all sorrows; the ocean laments on behalf of all those who suffer.' In the same extract he acknowledged the siren call of the sea on a sunny day, when the 'grandiose hilarity of a clear sky spreads over the sea', and 'the whole immensity of the ocean is a caress, and the waves sigh, and the reefs sing and the seaweed kisses the rock' and so forth. But of course this letter-writer did not throw the bottle into the sea on a balmy summer's day.

I turned to another of Hugo's works, *The Man Who Laughs*. The story is set on the English coast on a stormy January night in 1690. Pirates escaping from a raid abandon their latest victim, a child whom their 'diabolic surgery has transformed into a monster destined as a fairground amusement'. With their knives they had carved a big happy grin into the child's face. However, retribution stalks the pirate ship, for she immediately runs into a succession of terrible storms. The ship begins to founder and all hope of escape or rescue is abandoned.

The ship's doctor advises the rest of the crew: 'Let us throw our crimes into the sea. They are weighing on us. That is what is sinking the ship. Let us not think about rescue any more, let us think about our salvation . . .' He writes a note explaining their crime, and the torchlight illuminates the pale faces of the multinational band of sailors. Occasional sobs break the silence. The ship continues to sink.

They all sign their names to the document, one of the sailors drains the last drop of brandy from the flask, and then they slide the roll of paper into it, plug up the neck and seal it with tar. 'Now we will die,' announces the doctor and hurls the torch overboard. In the ensuing darkness all kneel down to pray, except for the doctor, silhouetted against the swirling snowflakes. The water rises to the shoulders of the kneeling men. As the doctor leads the prayers, each crew member cries 'Your will be done' in his own language. At the last response, there is only silence. The doctor lowers his eyes. He sees that all the men's heads are under water; not one had been raised. In their remorse, they had let themselves drown on their knees. The doctor takes the flask and raises it above his head. The ship sinks, and as he begins to disappear beneath the waves, the doctor continues to murmur the rest of the prayer. His chest remains above the water for a moment, then only his head, then there is just his arm holding the flask, as though showing it to infinity.

The arm disappears. The sea is now still and calm and the sinking ship scarcely leaves a ripple on its oily surface. The snow continues to fall.

But something floats on in the silent sea, moving on the current in the shadows. It is the sealed flask floating safely in its willow casing. Eventually this message in a bottle will reveal the identity of the sailors' young victim, and he will take up his rightful position in the House of Lords.

The grandfather of all these nineteenth-century ocean lovers was Jules Michelet (1798–1874), who wrote in his *Journal* that he conceived the idea of his major work, *The Sea*, as he pulled out from his wife after sex. Pages and pages of vividly described waves, beaches, currents and storms followed. He spoke of the ocean as a 'sea of milk', whitish and viscous, which hinted at its non-translucent, life-giving, seminal or maternal properties. But he did have a worthy respect for the sea as an immovable frontier between two spheres of existence, an invisible obstacle that had provided an unfranchizable transparent wall for the letter-writer too: 'Water, for all terrestrial beings, is the non-breatheable element, the element of asphyxiation. It is the fatal, eternal barrier, that irremediably separates the two worlds.' In a similar way the bottle with its letter was now separated from its sender by its journey through the water.

The Professor had been right. Not only was the language of the letter-writer influenced by Hugo and his contemporaries, but the whole 'letter-in-a-bottle' concept was very close to the hearts of these bearded men. Eleven years before Hugo's *Man who Laughs*, Alfred de Vigny, soldier and son of a soldier, wrote a long poem called *Letter in a Bottle*, with the subtitle *Advice to an Unknown Young Man*.

It tells of a young captain whose ship is out of control. No vessel appears to save them, night falls, he is resigned to his fate. He writes a note:

Today the current is dragging us eastwards, we are lost, on to Tierra del Fuego. Our death is certain. We should go north. Herewith I attach my journal with some studies of new constellations from distant latitudes. Where it lands, is in God's hands.

As the vessel begins to spin towards its destruction, the captain places his notes in an old champagne bottle, its green neck yellowed by ancient bubbles, from Rheims. He remembers when he toasted his friends from this bottle. Of three hundred crew members, only ten remain. The water is already up to his knees and soon it reaches his shoulders . . . Like the ship's doctor in Hugo's novel, he lifts one bare arm towards the sky. As his boat sinks, he throws the bottle. He smiles as he imagines the fragile glass carrying his name and his thoughts to port. A new star will be named after him, and he is happy to think that with his bottle he has tricked death.

The young captain's bottle floats along in the ocean, surviving currents, icebergs, black sea horses. Once, in the calm sea of the Pacific, amid blue waves, a boat passes. The bottle is spotted, a small dinghy is launched to pick it up. But suddenly, from afar, comes the gunfire of pirates. The dinghy is summoned back urgently to the ship, and she sails on swiftly to escape capture. Our hopes – the readers' hopes – were raised and now they are dashed.

Alone in the ocean, lost like an invisible dot in a moving desert, the bottle floats on, its neck now covered with algae and wrack.

At last the winds blow from Florida and bring the bottle to France – where else? – and its rainy shores. A fisherman spots it trapped beneath some rocks and runs to find a wise man to explain his catch.

The wise man explains that the information in the bottle is the elixir of science, of knowledge, for 'The true God, God almighty, is the God of ideas.'

The young captain had done well to consign his knowledge to the waves, and the poem ends:

Let us throw the letter into the sea, the teeming sea:
God will gently guide it to harbour.

Perhaps these overblown romantic tales of letters in bottles, cast by heroic men sinking gradually beneath the waves, arms upraised like the Statue of Liberty, sounded better in French, or perhaps better when read in a previous century. And yet the real letter, Maurice's mother's letter, was genuinely romantic. It had something of that wild Heathcliffean melodrama about it. But I had come across no direct borrowings, I had recognized no lines lifted from an earlier source, and I was no nearer to my self-imposed goal. It was time to try a different tack.

14

I sat before my telephone with the orange notelet that the artist had given me and prepared to contact the three people she had recommended.

Graphology, the study of handwriting. It seemed to me that it could tell me the mother's age, temperament, maybe even her country or region of origin. Ancient Jews, Romans and Chinese were aware that character could be revealed by an individual's handwriting, and early writings on the subject can be found in seventeenth-century Italy. Modern graphology is considered to date from the work of a circle of nineteenth-century French Catholic clergymen based around the Archbishop of Cambrai. The term itself was coined by the Abbé Jean-Hippolyte Michon (1806–81) who founded the Society of Graphology in Paris in 1871 and wrote several treatises on the subject, establishing the pre-eminence of the French in this field. Famous amateurs such as Thomas Gainsborough, Edgar Allan Poe, Robert Browning and Johann Wolfgang von Goethe were attracted by the study of hand-writing and helped to publicize its uses.

Graphology has remained on the fringes of scientific acceptability, often classified with phrenology and physiognomy. One of the leading forensic analysts of documents and forgeries admitted that it could provide revealing clues to a person's character, although 'Support is spare for graphology's claim that handwriting accurately reflects personality variables.' Earlier experts, however, had agreed that 'Every time a person writes he automatically and subconsciously stamps his individuality in his writing.' It certainly reveals something of where one learned to write. The letter-writer had a definitely French style of handwriting; the Professor had commented on it, and I too had immediately identified it as being similar to the writing of several French friends of mine, and very different from German handwriting, or my own English script. Individual characters are differently formed in the various national scripts, but would graphology be sophisticated enough to be able, for instance, to tell whether the writer was French or a French-speaking Belgian? It was far from being an exact science, even in France where it retained most credibility, but perhaps the general impressions one could derive from a study of handwriting were less elusive than quantifying the exact scientific accuracy of graphology. Whether or not I was going to get any answers that would help me track down the letter-writer was unclear, but I thought I would probably be offered some insights into her character and motivation. Perhaps that was becoming just as important as finding her.

The graphologist lived in a small high-rise block on the outskirts of Paris. She was a poet, and her small flat was full of flowers and scraps of paper covered in short scribbled phrases. It suited her, a bright, small woman, dressed in a floral print, with a hint of fragility behind the gaiety.

We made our introductions, and I opened the Evian bottle. I had not touched the original letter since first reading it, and had never even opened the bottle since my friend the dog-walker passed it on to me. For all my investigations, I used a colour photocopy I had made when I first received the letter. But the graphologist needed to see the original paper, the pressure of the pen, the texture of the script, so we carefully unrolled the little cylinder and straightened out the sheets. The lock of hair was twisted into a curl, and appropriately formed the shape of a question mark. It was impossible to tell whether the original was curly or whether the shape had been imposed by the paper scroll. We stared at the lock in shocked silence. Suddenly it was

obvious that there were two people's hair entwined together like lovers. A light chestnut and a dark brown.

The graphologist shuddered and blew out her cheeks in an effort to relax. The small noise released the tension in the room that had gripped us both. She seemed to clear her thoughts, and picked up the letter. 'It's very compact, very well-organized,' she said immediately, trying to sound businesslike after the emotional silence. 'There is a great respect for the norms: the margins are very crisp, especially the one on the left. It shows a great desire for clarity, there is nothing casual about it. It shows little imagination. Lots of control, a great desire for mastery. It is very organized,' she repeated. 'Precise, rigorous, it shows continuity, perseverance . . . She is tenacious, she follows through on what she has decided to do. It reveals cohesion, definition. It is very compact, very dense.'

She thought for a while. 'There is something obsessive, depressive, monotonous in the writing. It is almost suffocating in its own space.' She indicated the blue inked spaces and the contrasting white empty ones. 'The white is what is not spoken,' she explained. 'It is linked to listening, to the subconscious. The subconscious is very – perhaps too – controlled.'

She pointed out that the letter had been written with a line guide, a page with thick black lines placed behind the writing paper, to steer the pen into parallel correctness. The French expression was 'un guide âne', a donkey guide. The writer had used either an ink pen or a high-quality rollerball, though the graphologist thought it was more likely to be the former. She had whited out a mistake. This was not a letter written on a cliff-top in a howling gale of emotion. This was a letter probably drafted beforehand and certainly written on the correct stationery at a table.

'The writer has a relatively high level of education,' continued the graphologist, 'although she does make some elementary spelling mistakes, some grammatical errors. The occasional verb did not agree, perhaps because she was writing with such emotion, perhaps simply because she was an erratic speller.

147

'She is quite introverted, a woman who keeps things back. The graphologist pointed to the tiny upward-shooting ends of many of the words. These, she said, are among the least modifiable elements of handwriting. 'She seems very controlled, it appears to be all very disciplined, but then there is a reactive, almost a violent dimension. She presents a very calm façade but underneath it all she is bubbling with emotion. It is almost as though she is not authorized to be spontaneous but even so there are these little explosive episodes. It is as though she is trying very hard to master her emotions. Her pleasure principle is very restrained, very bridled. I'm not convinced that she achieved an inner freedom.

'There is a touch of guilt here, maybe an element of masochism. An obsessional neurosis perhaps. She has had a very organized life, without much scope for imagination. She gives the impression of calm, but within her there is a tempest. Either life or her education has flattened her spirit, but deep down she is animated, vibrant, alive.'

At the top left-hand corner of each page sat the sideways sloping eight, the sign of infinity. At the beginning and end of the letter were two V shapes, like a symbol for a tick or a symbolic seagull. The graphologist thought these were birds, and I vaguely recalled that in the Kevin Costner film his notepaper had some kind of seagull image at the head. Maybe the writer was trying to emulate the film, just as she had lifted some phrases from it. Or perhaps that reflected the desire for freedom, the metaphorical rise from water through to the air of the letter's imagery.

'The density of the text implies that she may be unable to distance herself from her emotions. Her judgement may be affected by this excess of emotions, by her inability to withdraw.' The graphologist pointed to the way the loops of the lines overlapped, which had led her to draw this conclusion. The 'g' of 'infatigablement' in line 17 was mingled with the 'f' of 'froid' in the following line, and this was frequently repeated throughout the letter. 'Certainly she has an important need to express herself, a need to talk, to unburden herself, even before her son.'

désirs, un trop vif de vivance, à l'aurore de l'été. Il a voyagé longtemps entre deux caux, entre deux lumières, pour tenter d'éteindre infatigablement le repos de ses deux bras tendus. Il a subi, le silence, les peurs et le froid,

I asked her how old she thought the letter-writer might be. 'It is not a juvenile handwriting. She is certainly not adolescent, but I would not have thought she was very old either. It is a conventional script. Her writing shows a certain vitality,' she continued. 'She is not disorientated by sickness or medication. There is a healthy tension in the writing.

'She is intelligent, precise, rigorous. She seems to have a feeling for numbers, perhaps she is an accountant. There is a sense of accomplishment. There is no amateurism here. She is not a superficial person. She depends on her past experience. She is a woman of today, but she needs her points of reference. I see no sign of the nomad – this is not someone who would grab her rucksack and go off round the world. She needs her everyday security. She needs some kind of solid structure in her life.'

By now the graphologist was well and truly in her stride. 'She seems nice at first, very gentle, but I think she could be authoritarian if you lived with her. She is not easy to influence. She is basically sensitive, but also – it seems to me – quite touchy, on her dignity. The writing perhaps shows a failure to listen enough. There is an anal dimension to her, in the Freudian sense, and also quite a masculine side to her. It seems to me that the style of writing is rather masculine. There are not many signs of femininity here.

'She is brave, dignified, faithful. Not great fun, but you can rely on her. Her writing reveals a certain presence, but she is sometimes awkward, not at ease with her space, there is not a great deal of comfort in the writing.'

The graphologist kept returning to the one overriding impression, the sense of a thick, almost suffocating layer of control, plastered over an emotional cauldron. But unless I found the letter-writer, how would I know whether this was a convincing description of a precise, well-organized, obsessive, repressed, sensitive, serious, faithful, courageous woman or just the ramblings of a well-meaning amateur?

We re-twirled the hair into its nest within the letter, scrolled the paper carefully just the way it was and repacked everything into the bottle among the perfumed sandalwood shavings. The graphologist was almost reluctant to let me go. Like many others whose I advice I had asked, she had somehow been touched by the unknown woman's plight, and she wanted to know the end of the story.

I moved on to the next contact on the orange notelet, the folli-cologist, the 'bulbologue'. The three contacts from the artist – graphologist, follicologist and tarot reader – had been offered in a secluded garden in the outskirts of Paris on what had turned out to be a special evening. In French, *graphologue, bulbologue, tarologue* . . . the list had seemed to offer an alluring magic spell that would solve the mystery without resorting to the vulgarity of an appeal in the media.

However, contact with the follicologist was almost immediately unproductive. I had hoped he would be able to tell me how old the hair was, or the boy's age when the lock was cut. I had even begun to fantasize that he could find trace elements of drugs in the hair, which might have explained how 'he slipped away from life in an excess of desires, too full of vivid life'. The assistant mentioned that the analyst could check bone density, stress levels, hormonal imbalances . . . But it was not to be. The hair had, of course, not been torn out by the roots, but carefully snipped in mid-strand. My friend the dog-walker had found it strange that a loving mother should throw away a lock of hair from her son. At any rate, I received a courteous letter from the follicologist:

Dear Madame,

I am sorry to say that my expertise is only relevant if the root of the hair is present. With the follicles, one could find chromosomes to analyse family relations, minerals to reveal where the person lived if they had stayed in the same geographic area for long enough.

I suggest you talk to some television shows and perhaps the mother will come forward. I think she is hoping for just that, since at the moment she doesn't know that the bottle has been found. It would doubtless comfort her to share her grief. And if she talks about it, perhaps it would help her grieving process.

'Talk to some television shows' sounded deceptively simple. It seemed to me that the locks of hair must offer some clues, perhaps from a more mainstream analyst than this follicologist cum bereavement counsellor.

On every French high street, and especially in the wealthy part of Paris where I stayed and where the population tended to be elderly, there are laboratories offering medical analysis, where people can bring in a blood or urine sample and have it checked. I asked whether they could do a DNA sample on a lock of hair. The receptionist, fiddling with her silvery watch strap, confirmed what the follicologist had said, that it was impossible. One cannot do DNA samples on hair because there are no cells. When I questioned this, uncertain of my hazy scientific knowledge, she assured me, patting her own elaborate, cell-free coiffure into place, that she was a highly qualified biologist and knew she was right.

It seemed to me that with a lock of hair – even without follicles – and surely some skin or saliva cells somewhere in the bottle, some trace DNA would be present. I realized that I was basing this conclusion on late nights watching American forensic police thrillers.

In an attempt to discover whether an analysis of the DNA in a lock of hair would bring me any closer to discovering the identity of Maurice or his mother, I started to read up on the process. DNA stands for deoxyribonucleic acid. In 1984 Alec Jeffreys, a geneticist at

Leicester University, announced his findings on DNA fingerprinting, a term he soon patented. As early as December 1985, another scientific breakthrough – PCR, polymerase chain reaction – meant that minute quantities of DNA could be copied and amplified, so that scientists could provide themselves with enough material with which to carry out forensic investigations. These breakthroughs meant that even a tiny trace of the stuff could help to identify or eliminate suspects by determining each individual's unique genetic code.

The implications of DNA and PCR soon became evident. Barry Scheck, later to become even more famous as the DNA expert on O. J. Simpson's defence team, co-founded the Innocence Project to investigate suspect verdicts. 'We always knew that there had to be innocent people in jail and that their innocence could be proved through DNA,' said Scheck. 'But people didn't realize then – and still don't – how amazingly powerful the technology is. Prosecutors, defence lawyers, forensic scientists, let alone the prisoners and their families don't know . . . that this cup you're drinking from will have saliva on it, from which DNA can be extracted. They don't know that you can get it from the sweat on the headband of a hat. They don't know you can gender-type a bloodstain.' They probably do by now.

For hair to contain DNA, the root did need to be present. But mitochondrial DNA – mtDNA – was present in all cells, although not in the nuclei, which meant that any cellular material, such as a hair shaft, should contain it. It was this method that had been used in 1994 to check whether Anna Anderson had really been Princess Anastasia Romanov, the last descendant of the Russian Tsar. The 'highly qualified biologist' had been wrong. Although there probably was no DNA present in locks of hair, there would be mtDNA, and this was passed from mother to child, or more specifically from mother to son. And, I thought, the locks of hair enclosed with the letter must surely belong to Maurice and his mother.

At this point I decided to contact a forensic scientist to see if this investigative path would lead anywhere. She explained that she did work with hair shafts with no follicles, but that her analysis was done on a comparative basis, she never provided definite answers. In her work at the Forensic Science Service she was sent all the evidence from a scene of crime but this was often no more than a single hair.

There were certain disadvantages with my two locks of hair, she told me. Firstly, the mtDNA would presumably be identical in both samples – unless Maurice was not the biological son of the letter-writer, which seemed unlikely. And secondly, she would not even be able to tell me which lock was from which person. Or even whether they were from two different people. Hair colour was not relevant. 'My husband, for instance,' she said to underline the point, 'has two very blond patches in a darker head of hair.'

Seeing my disappointment, she consoled me by telling me that her true area of speciality was balaclavas, as worn by criminals to hide their faces, and I should really contact a true hair specialist. I grasped at the offered straw.

The recommended hair specialist, a leader in his field, had worked on the case of the woman who had for many years falsely claimed to be Princess Anastasia Romanov. Sadly, he confirmed everything that the forensic scientist had told me. The evidence – hair shafts possibly from two unknown people – was insufficient. If Maurice had a criminal record, there might be some chance of distinguishing between them, but French databases were apparently at a far less advanced level than in the UK (as I already knew), and even if I found some way to access these, I was told, there were no police mtDNA databases.

Without a comparative reference, the locks of hair were useless from an investigative point of view. Once I found the source of the hair, the specialist consoled me, he would be able to double-check whether this was indeed the case. But, by then, I would no longer need his help.

15

My research until now had yielded little information. It had turned into a process by which I crossed possibilities off the list, rather than leading anywhere. Through Evian I had discovered approximately when the bottle was produced, and the film that Maurice's mother had watched. But the tidal patterns were close to useless, the registry offices were hopeless; DNA provided no information, graphology and literary analysis gave insights but no real progress; internet research was ongoing but not hopeful. I picked up the orange notelet with the last telephone number on it.

I rang the tarot reader. I had never consulted the tarot, and my opinion of its usefulness would offend any believer. And yet intelligent friends used it and even practised it. The artist had given me the telephone number with a sense of certainty that I would be helped, and I found the temptation irresistible. Was there any possibility that this was not mumbo jumbo?

As we talked on the phone I could hear paperwork being shuffled in the background. When I told the tarot reader what I was ringing about she was clearly astonished. She told me that for the last two decades she had been searching for a woman, her own mother, whose clock and tiny notebook she had found. Abandoned as a baby, she had finally tracked down her mother and had just written a book about her search. It was this manuscript that I could hear her stuffing into an envelope to send off to a publisher even as we spoke. She was incredulous that on the day she had finished her quest, I should call about another – she thought, amazingly similar – one.

When I read her the final lines of the letter – 'This letter, my son, I intend to share with only one person, the only friend I will keep all my life, and beyond. She is called Christine, she is gentleness itself' – the tarot reader gasped.

'Christine – that's *my* name!' she cried. Although I knew she was called Christine it hadn't really struck me as significant. 'Incredible,' she exclaimed. 'It's a sign. It was meant to be.'

She asked whether any children in my family had died, which she said would tend to prove the link between the letter-writer and myself. I said no, apart from in Auschwitz. It was a silly remark, no sooner uttered than regretted. She seized on this, however, and asked if there were any Jewish clues in the letter. I told her there were references to lotus blossoms and seagulls, which were not Jewish motifs. The tarot reader was undaunted. 'But your ancestors did die young,' she insisted. I pointed out somewhat acidly that everyone's ancestors are dead, many of them young, and made a conscious effort to curb the scepticism that was threatening to overwhelm me. Like everyone else I had consulted about the letter, she was reading her favourite interpretation into it.

This call was proving to be as unscientific as I had feared. But as I needed all the help I could get, I felt I should explore every avenue, whether in this dimension or the next.

'It's a triangle,' the tarot reader announced. 'The lady, you and your friend the dog-walker. But I'm linked, too, because of the book I've been writing, and because of my name.'

I bit back the obvious retort that a four-cornered triangle is a rectangle and we arranged to meet the following day.

The tarot reader's room was small, clean, with white walls, and three small paintings behind her chair, clearly created by the artist who had put me in touch with her. They were the same glowing blue as the painting I had bought, and the small squiggly symbols, she told me, represented the father, the mother and the child. They looked vaguely spermatozoid. She had a comfortable housewifely and almost rotund face and manner, and I felt slightly short-changed, as though a tarot reader ought to operate in a dank, dim-lit cell or shadowed tent and look more like something from the Addams family.

I handed her the bottle, since she told me she would need to feel the lady through the bottle and the letter. She was amazed at its beauty. For her, it represented a breast, a feeding bottle, a drop of milk. Evian's design department would have despaired. It was a symbol of life, she said, a shape specially designed to attract women with children. 'It evokes maternity in its purest form,' she rhapsodized. The woman who chose this bottle, she said, was flirtatious, joyous. Did she buy the bottle after writing the letter; or did she buy the bottle and then write the letter? Was it a bottle for a letter, or a letter for a bottle? Either way she had chosen a happy object, a sparkling and luminous thing. Blue and golden. (With a large brand name on it, I mentally added.)

Then she began to shuffle the cards. She used a pack of twenty-two cards, the Major Arcana, which are supposed to represent the major turning points in our lives: our commitments, triumphs and tragedies. She began by asking the cards about the letter-writer's life. The first card to be drawn was the Sun, a very positive one. Her childhood had been happy, she announced, there was a firm, joyful foundation. Then, during the second stage of her life, worries had

emerged. There had been problems linked to men, to sexuality, to money. She had become blocked, had not known how to go on living. All had been black and terrible. Then there had been a change. There was a third stage, where she was united to a companion, possibly married . . . at any rate living with someone. She was still alive, and she had experienced some form of resurrection, of transformation. The tarot reader thought for a moment. The letter-writer had great reserves of energy and vitality, she added.

What is the woman like? she asked. The cards responded that physically she was graceful and slight, that there was a lightness about her, perhaps a resemblance to a young man, a slightly androgynous element. She moved about a great deal, perhaps she had a job that involved physical movement in some way. She was dynamic, energetic. Both she and the bottle bubbled with gaiety, explained the tarot reader. She had the sun within her. She had known paradise. She had a sort of radiance. Whenever the tarot reader asked about the woman, the cards for the Sun and Temperance seemed to appear.

Where was the lady when she threw the bottle? The card for the Hermit appeared. She was very lonely, and alone when she threw the bottle. Then the card of Death appeared, suggesting that throwing the bottle into the sea had coincided with a period of mourning. The mourning was not necessarily short, but she had emerged from it very suddenly and had learned to live with her grief. There had been a difficult period where she had abandoned all hope, a period of complete nothingness, but after casting forth the bottle, she was now ready to deal with life. If there is a companion, as the Emperor's card hinted, he is a more stable, older man. Maybe she had already known him previously; he was far more reliable than the man from the earlier relationship.

Is there another child? The cards apparently refused to answer. Maurice himself was very alone, said the tarot reader. He did not die quickly, suddenly. There seemed to be many elements appearing, and she studied the cards for a long time. Perhaps there were difficulties identifying him? At all events the process leading to his death had been long and difficult. The problems seemed to have sprung from his father, or perhaps from the lack of one. The chronological root of his difficulties was definitely the absence of his father. This, she said, was the source of all the later problems. Did the tarot reader see this in the cards, or did she guess it from the letter? Or was she making use of such information as was available, either from the letter or from my inadvertent clues. Was this the very nature of the tarot?

When she asked about his death, the pleasant cards seemed to disappear. Justice, Death, the Devil and the Hanged Man appeared. Maurice had experienced a violent crisis, she said. It was physical rather than psychological. It was his body that was affected. She emphasized the violence. She couldn't decide if it was a disease or an accident, but she was sure that it was violent. He had felt very alone at the time of his death.

Maurice and his mother had lived together almost as a couple, rather than as parent and child. He had replaced his father in her life and felt responsible for her. He had matured quickly, and had acted as her companion, wanting to protect her. He saw his mother as a woman who needed protection.

Next came the Magician and the Madman cards, showing someone gifted but unstable. The son had tried many things in his life. He was 'all fire and flames', he would try anything once.

The tarot reader picked up the bottle again. Perhaps she had thrown the bottle on his birthday. Why had she chosen that particular day? The cards seemed to indicate that Maurice was born under the sign of Aries, but that would put his birthday between 21 March and 19 April which unfortunately did not fit chronologically with Evian's production dates for the bottle. At all events the tarot reader was convinced that the mother definitely wanted it to be found and analysed. The bottle was too attractive to have been bought only to carry the letter through the water.

I finally realized that I, too, could put direct questions to the tarot – or at least to the tarot reader. Did Maurice die of a disease? I asked. Yes, came the response. His body was hit by fire, especially on the head. Perhaps it was a violent migraine, a fever. Or maybe a fractured skull, a cerebral haemorrhage. A violent blow? The cards were ambivalent as to the cause, although the Chariot card seemed to indicate a road accident. His mother was present at his death, or during the event that precipitated it. Perhaps, after suffering a violent blow, he died slowly of an inflammation. At the actual time of his death, Maurice experienced a moment of grace, a kind of luminosity.

I was beginning to flag. The cards seemed to offer a definite response but on closer inspection they wrapped themselves again in ambiguity. How could I rely on their responses?

I yielded to wicked temptation and asked for some details about the letter-writer's address. I was firmly frowned upon.

Did Maurice drown? I asked. No, said the Hermit card very definitely.

Did he kill himself? No.

Was it a drug overdose? Maybe, came the response. It is possible, but not obvious. Probably not, but it was something excessive. The tarot reader saw an element of imprudence, a lack of control. This imprudence had perhaps caused the illness that led to his death. He had died of excess, but not of drugs. He had rushed in somewhere and lost control, said the Chariot and the Devil cards. There was no water involved. He was a turbulent, mischievous, headstrong boy. His cards seemed to be the Magician and the Fool. Above the magician's head was the same symbol as the letter-writer had drawn in the top left-hand corners of each sheet of paper.

The graphologist had pointed out the sideways eight of the infinity symbol but it had not made any particular impression on me. Now that I saw this symbol above the magician's head it seemed to me to be significant. Maybe Maurice's mother was interested in tarot; maybe the cards did possess some secret accuracy.

Did she throw the bottle out to sea from the coast or from a boat? There was no boat involved, came the response. After some hesitation, she had climbed to a high place, maybe even somewhere risky, and thrown it from the top of a cliff. In this way she integrated Maurice's death into her own flesh. She lived through it as though it was her own death, the Magician and the Hanged Man cards said. Now she is a strong survivor, having been transformed by her experience. The two elements, the mother and son, the Temperance card and the Magician card, are linked by solitude. Hers seemed to be the Temperance card, signifying balance, the healing effects of time.

Did she live near the sea when she cast the bottle? The cards refused to answer. They had had enough and, quite suddenly, so had I.

The certainty and fluency of the interpretation was quite convincing, but until I found the letter-writer, I would be unable to ascertain the accuracy of any of the tarot reader's statements. The fact that she had used the infinity symbol in the corner of her pages was interesting and probably indicated a familiarity with the world of tarot. If I trusted the cards, I would perhaps start looking for a beach with a sheer cliff somewhere along the French coast, but apart from the vagueness of the clue, I simply could not trust the information enough to rule out the alternatives. It had been interesting and quite amusing, but I remained sceptical about the value of the tarot.

If you're consulting the tarot, Christine had said, you are strongly advised to consult the stars as well. Bemused, I agreed. The astrologer asked for my date of birth, the hour, and my ascendant zodiac sign. I also needed the birth details of my dog-walking friend, since the initial contact with the letter came through her. The astrological results, I was assured, would be significant. I hung up and contacted my friend. We both rang our mothers who struggled to remember the details of our arrivals in this world. Fully informed, I rang back to commission our charts to be read in conjunction, somehow, with the bottle.

I was unconvinced that astrology would bring me closer to finding the writer of the letter, but being led through this wonderland of spiritual novelty made me feel that I was still searching. Perhaps in a small, quiet corner of myself I was hopeful that against all the odds the tarot cards or the stars would point me in the right direction. Or perhaps I simply wanted to feel that I had left no stone unturned.

I had told the astrologer that – in vain as it turned out – I did not want any psychological insights into my own character or predictions about what the future held for me personally. She was to concentrate on the bottle. Consultations took place in a little office in the garden used only for that purpose. She was building up her astrological practice, and meanwhile she was a very successful, high-flying family lawyer. Her husband was a businessman, and almost aggressively dubious about her work. She was very clinical, she told me; she would present her findings in a strictly analytical manner.

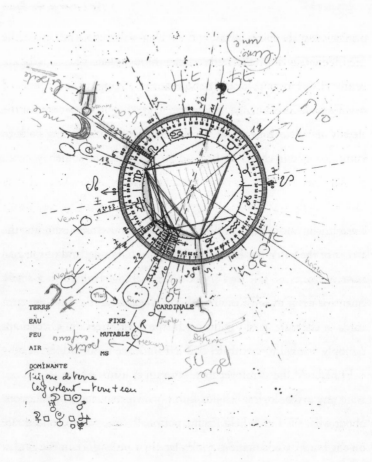

She handed me my chart. My horizon apparently was bounded by my parents, father and mother at each end. The presence of Uranus and the moon in Leo showed that the education of children was very important to me, whether that of my own children or in a more general way. Privately I agreed – I had just written a book about a particular aspect of education, and always worried about my own children's educational progress – but I did not enlighten her. The planets in my Fifth House apparently showed a great concern for aspects of dealing with children, the family, parenthood. 'The sky at your birth already revealed this, which struck me immediately,' the astrologer said.

My friend's chart was the mirror image of mine. Our planets showed many points of convergence, creating a strong relationship between us, but her experiences of motherhood were more problematic than mine. We both had the same sensitivity towards all family matters, which would explain why, astrologically speaking, she had entrusted me with the bottle. I objected, pointing out that I was probably the only friend of the dog-walker's who knew French, certainly the only one with whom she was exchanging three work phone calls a day. The astrologer brushed my comments aside.

She became very animated as she drew connecting lines between my planets. When she had linked Saturn, Neptune, Pluto and the moon, even I could see the symmetrical shape of a kite emerging. I asked whether everyone had a similar image on their chart, and she obligingly joined up my friend's lines, which made nothing in the least symmetrical or recognizable. The kite meant that, even at my birth, I would be sending messages into the sky; there would be something childish, magical, about my efforts. The kite was a link between the earth and the water, soaring into the air. In my mind's eye I saw Mary Poppins' bankers standing on Primrose Hill shouting, 'Let's go fly a kite.' The astrologer was on a different plane altogether: 'Symbolically this links you to the message, to maternity, to paternity,' she said. 'Only the letter-writer uses the sea, you use the air.' And she added, 'That is the clinical truth.'

Then she went through each of my planets, using the Sabian symbols, which are apparently symbolic pictures meant to arouse a realization of the power of one's own creative spirit. These pictures, or degrees, I later found out, had been 'manifested' as a kind of 'contemporary American I Ching' by Marc Edmund Jones and Miss Elsie Wheeler in San Diego's Balboa Park in 1925, and later reworked by Dane Rudhyar in his book *The Astrology of Personality*, first published in 1936. Nearly forty years later, Rudhyar wrote *An Astrological Mandala* in which, by using 'a more holistic and humanistic approach, [he] promoted the idea of using the Sabian symbols as an oracle'. It was interesting to see a French astrologer drawing on Western as well as Eastern cultures in an effort to reach an accurate interpretation. From Confucius to trailer park.

Each planet referred to a specific Sabian symbol or phrase, which could of course be interpreted in many ways. Mercury, the planet of early infancy, produced 'A young child learns to walk, encouraged by its parents.' Pluto was a merry-go-round. Both were childish symbols, and when I challenged the astrologer rather aggressively to tell me the neighbouring phrases, to see if they were also childish, she told me that the previous symbol was a harem, and the following one was 'a young couple go window-shopping', neither of which, I had to agree, carried the remotest overtones of childhood.

We returned to the planets. Uranus, which represented freedom, told me that 'A carrier pigeon accomplishes its mission.' Another astrological conjunction produced 'A woman waters the flowers in her garden,' and I thought of the flowers and plants wilting in my garden and allotment back home while I was far away on a fruitless quest. Scorpio uncannily gave 'The rescue of a drowning man.' Leo: 'Absorbed by his interior research, a seated man meditates without paying any attention to his appearance,' and I thought of several men in my life who could fit that description. And then the black moon spat out, 'A young black woman fights for her rights,' and my scepticism returned.

This black moon was the only element above my horizon, and therefore the only force of which I was apparently truly conscious. The position of the planets revealed a curiosity without limits. I would go to the furthest extent, said the astrologer, to hunt out the most complicated of things, the most mysterious, the most fantastic. This curiosity was now linked, not only to my desire for freedom but to my spiritual search, to an interrogation into the very nature of death. This seemed profound, but as the astrologer was aware of my quest to trace the origins of the bottle, her deductions about my abnormal levels of curiosity were not entirely intuitive. And as the astrologer pointed out, the phrases were all symbolic and could be interpreted in so many different ways. As the Sabian website stated: 'Like all Oracles, whichever answer you find is the one you need.'

The astrologer pulled her conclusions together. I was a messenger. I had a great desire for freedom, I had a boundless curiosity, I had a great urge to protect children, and somehow this protective aim had a masculine element to it. I had a subconscious strength and gifts that would link me with the needs of other people. I could pass on subconscious messages that would abolish distances. I had been releasing metaphorical kites all my life, and since I had the capacity to receive messages thrown in the other direction, it was not surprising that I had received this letter in a bottle. The positions of Saturn and the black moon indicated that I was approaching a challenge never to be repeated. Most of the analysis was vaguely flattering and I could easily see where it slotted into the context of my current quest.

My friend the dog-walker's chart was more tentative. She was worried by the bottle; she lacked both the energy and the confidence to take on the search. It touched her too deeply, it was too personal. And, said the astrologer, she was psychologically imprisoned in some way and therefore unable to follow it through. But, though unhappy, she was a luminous person. She had passed the bottle on to me because she trusted me, although in general she didn't trust the world. And, added the astrologer in a misplaced rush of confidence, she probably had twins. I heaved a sigh of relief as my view of the scientific accuracy of astrology remained intact.

After consulting the astrologer and the tarot reader, and, to some extent, the graphologist, I felt I should concentrate my search on less alternative methodologies. The visits had been intriguing, but had produced no conclusions. I had become stuck in my quest, and had looked for some easy answers. Now I resolved to follow up some more conventional leads.

16

The British detective that I approached early on in the quest had offered to contact international counterparts through his membership of the World Association of Detectives but this had failed to provide any leads. I decided I could wait no longer for his help and contacted a French detective myself. The French Yellow Pages listed hundreds of private eyes and at random I selected *A bas l'abus* – Down with Abuse – for no other reason than that was near the front of the alphabet, and I liked the melody of the title.

The detective's secretary said he would be back at 2 p.m., so I sat and waited for his return to the office in the tiny, leafy Place de Commerce. This turned out to be the shortest meeting I had had so far during my quest. 'Madame, you simply do not have enough information,' he said as he showed me the door through which I had only just stepped. 'Your only chance is to publicize it on television. You have absolutely no hope otherwise.'

My first reaction was defiance that the man had not even had the courtesy to listen while I outlined the research I had already carried out, but since it was objectively true that it had left me none the wiser, he was – objectively speaking – right. By the time I opened the door and walked back out into the Place de Commerce, I was in a state of complete dejection.

Once again I was receiving advice I did not want to hear. I wanted to find the letter-writer privately, quietly, by my own efforts, and without the glare of publicity. It was becoming increasingly clear that it was unlikely to happen that way. But I kept on hoping that just a few more leads, a few more days, would bring the answer.

That night I dined with Parisian friends. An old college friend had risen up the ranks of the diplomatic service and reached a level where she was an adviser to a government minister, while her husband controlled vast budgets for erstwhile French colonies in Africa. They were intrigued by my quest and, on hearing of the summary treatment I had received earlier that day, tried to cheer me up by suggesting new avenues to explore. By the time the tiny but exquisitely cooked portions of fish had been replaced by an expertly tossed salad, they were recalling a mutual friend who was now a secret police chief. They would contact him and organize a meeting. I felt a surge of hope – at last some help, perhaps an entrée into sources of information not generally available to the public.

Apparently the chief ran a special investigative unit for a department of the French secret service that no one was allowed to know about. I arrived punctually for my meeting, hoping I was dressed elegantly enough to impress an important spy. The entrance to the office building near the Bastille was nondescript but the foyer was discreetly protected by cameras, burly receptionists and security codes. What does a French secret policeman look like? I wondered. Maybe I should have reread *The Day of the Jackal.* I was collected by a scruffy plainclothes man, wearing the sort of jeans and trainers you can run fast in and, although it was a very hot day, the sort of bulky jacket that can disguise a weapon. I tried to keep up in my smart high heels as he hurried me through several doors protected by PIN codes. I had had to walk miles already that day, and my comfortable shoes were secreted in my briefcase.

The secret police chief had a very big office. He wore a smart Armani-style suit, and smoked a large noxious cigar. He was tall, thin and elegant, with sad, rather anxious eyes. He shook my hand and immediately asked me to tell him the facts. As he had heard the story already from my friend, he wanted only a factual resumé from me – and very speedily. Since the facts were so sparse, this did not present a problem. I had the distinct impression that I had only a brief slot in his overcrowded timetable. As I fumbled to bring out the bottle, which I had brought with me in case he needed hard evidence of the truth of my tale, he summoned a deputy to sit in on the interview.

The deputy was a more down-to-earth type. In his early fifties, tubby, experienced, tough, he looked as though he had seen it all. He lit a cigarette and the fug of Gauloise and cigar smoke thickened the air and caught at my throat; I had the strangest sensation of having strayed into a *film noir*. The deputy twiddled his greying moustache as he listened to my bald statements. The first name, the age. 'Madame,' he said, echoing the French private detective, 'you simply don't have enough clues.'

The boss interrupted him. 'Madame is a good friend of a good friend,' he told his deputy with a meaningful look. 'We will do all we can to help.' The deputy refocused. 'It is not a question of money,' the boss added, raising his hand as though to wave away a bribe. I hid my surprise, since it had never occurred to me to offer one, and I would not have known how to go about suggesting it, or, given his expensive taste in suits, have been able to afford his charge. He started to read the letter while I summarized my efforts so far, brushing over the meetings with the astrologer and the tarot card reader.

When the deputy had finished reading the letter, he announced, 'I'm not convinced it's a crime.' I was convinced it wasn't a crime, but

I didn't want to block any possible angle of investigation. The boss rose to his feet. 'I don't make promises lightly,' he said grandly. 'But if you will send me an email with all the information you have, all your efforts so far, and where you would like us to help you, I will promise you to open all possible avenues of exploration.' And as he flourished his cigar towards me and I tried not to cough, I had the feeling that my case was as good as solved. The full resources of the secret policeman's department would be thrown into finding the writer of the letter and the cause of death of her son, Maurice. My important friends would be vindicated and the secret policeman's intellectual satisfaction and vanity would be assuaged.

The chief indicated that the meeting was over and I mumbled my delighted thanks. While I tried to scoop up the letter, the bottle, the packaging in which I had wrapped the bottle, my briefcase and my notebook, after attempting to shake hands with him and the deputy, he swiftly turned to some papers on his desk. Clutching my belongings I was escorted firmly from the room by the deputy. I could not help regretting that I was not leaving in a dignified and sophisticated manner as I repacked the bottle and rearranged the contents of my briefcase in the corridor, with the door to his office safely closed.

From: Karen Liebreich

To: X

Subject: Letter in a bottle

Dear M. X,

Thank you very much for offering to help track down
this mysterious lady, especially given how busy you
must be. I would be really grateful for any doors
you could open or advice, etc. Herewith the details
you requested from me:

A The facts

The concrete facts are sparse:

1. The son was called Maurice.

2. He was thirteen years old when he died.

3. He was her first son.

4. He died one summer evening, 'à l'aurore de
   l'été'.

5. Evian bottle, paper, ink, ribbon, two locks of
   hair.

6. She has a close friend called Christine, to whom
   she intends to show the letter.

Other clues are less concrete, maybe just metaphors?

1. 'sans prévenir, il s'est dérobé à la vie dans un

trop plein de désirs, un trop vif de vivance.' A
drug overdose? Driving his bike too recklessly?

2. 'Il a voyagé longtemps entre deux eaux, entre
deux lumières, pour tenter d'éteindre infatigablement le repos de ses deus bras tendus.' Did he
drown? Did he float in the sea? In a coma?

3. 'ce terrible moment où tu me glissais entre les
doigts . . .' So she was present at his death?

4. 'Mon fils a regagné le port, près d'un rivage
lointain, tout près du soleil levant.' Symbolic or
actual?

B My progress

1. INED told me the number of boys drowning between
the ages of 10 and 14 years. INSERM told me how
many of these commit suicide or die in accidents,
divided by regions of France. Neither of these
could give me further details about the individuals involved, nor could advise how to progress.
Now I am not sure that Maurice died by drowning.
Perhaps the references to floating, water, etc. are
literary rather than literal.

2. I visited a private detective, who told me about
ESDA (a special technique to investigate the
paper). I have not yet followed this up.

3. Evian told me the bottle was manufactured between October 2001 and the finding of the bottle, February 2002. The contact assures me she cannot discover where the bottle was sold, but I feel a visit may inspire her to check further, and I intend to go there.

4. News databases, as used by financial institutions, and the internet, have yielded no useful information.

5. Part of the first paragraph and the last paragraph uses lines from a Kevin Costner film, 'Message in a Bottle', released in 1999.

6. I read through the Nécrologie for Voix du Nord, for May and June for 1995–2000. No luck. I also read June 1995 for the following papers: 'Ouest France', 'Paris-Normandie', 'Nord-Éclair' before becoming discouraged.

7. I tried to get access to death certificates, but it seems these are not held centrally in France. I was told each mairie holds its own records, and permission is needed from the Procureur de la République to access these.

8. 'Analyse en bulbologie capillaire.' Unfortunately there are no roots to the hair, so he is unable to progress.

9. Graphologue. She has provided psychological 'insights' but no concrete information, other than that the woman is not very young, and not very old (maybe 35–55 years old).

10. Clinical psychologist. Says that the mourning period for a mother/child loss is at least two years.

11. Lifeboats at Sheppey, where the bottle was found. The captain suggests it could have been thrown in locally, or somewhere like Margate or Norfolk — but since the bottle was not for sale in the UK, I am dubious. Possibly thrown in from a cross-Channel ferry. From Dieppe eastwards, the current would be amenable, with a North-easterly wind. Oostende would also be possible. Further west, Cherbourg etc, the current would take the bottle in the opposite direction. The letter-writer says she will throw the bottle in 'au large des côtes'.

C What I would like to ask from you?

1. You mentioned a central register of deaths. Can one check if there is a record of Maurice's death? I am quite prepared to sit and trawl through the years, and to be discreet about the

source of information, if this is possible. This seems to me the most important thing.

2. Your deputy mentioned a database of dead people's DNA. Could one check that for Maurice, or check it against the DNA from the hair I have? But if it is only from the last 18 months, maybe that will be useless?

3. I would like to ask the police in the North of France if they have information about the death of this 13-year-old. Any helpful contacts?

4. What about making contact with the lifeguards, magistrates, hospitals?

5. Are there other technical procedures, such as ESDA, which could be done on the letter or the hair?

6. Can you suggest other avenues of research that I should follow?

I appreciate that these are a lot of questions, and I will quite understand if you are too busy. I would be very grateful for any suggestions, leads, contacts, etc that you could offer.

Yours sincerely

Karen Liebreich

I waited a few weeks and when this email produced no response I sent another and also telephoned the police chief's office. I even hinted, in the most delicate way, that I would be prepared to fund some additional research, for instance, if someone other than me had to sit and sift through database entries of adolescent deaths. The emails went unanswered; my calls were always fobbed off by a secretary. I never heard from the police chief again, and my diplomatic friends felt unable to pursue the subject when they next met him.

Perhaps he realized that it was a task beyond his abilities, but then why not send me a polite terminal rebuff? I could only assume that the offer had been bullshit, part of some kind of personal fantasy that he could solve all mysteries. It was a very disappointing outcome after my hopes had been raised.

I knew that the time had come either to abandon the search or to take it more seriously. I turned back to my work, to my children, but found it hard to concentrate on other matters. The letter would not leave me in peace – it was like an itch that had to be scratched. Once again I found I could not give up the quest so easily; there were still a few loose threads left hanging from my earlier enquiries. A little more investigation would surely help to tie them up.

17

The first private detective had mentioned ESDA (Electronic Static Detection Analysis) and I had yet to follow his suggestion up. It required specialist equipment and an experienced forensic detective. When I rang the private eye to see if he could organize something, he was clearly preoccupied, but hurriedly provided me with the details of a laboratory in central London, adding that his name should not be mentioned.

The forensic detective's offices were in an anonymous block near Victoria Station, a brisk five-minute walk from the Houses of Parliament. A solid-looking security guard stopped me at the entrance. 'Are you a policewoman?' he enquired. I wasn't sure whether to be flattered or offended. 'No,' I replied, wondering if I would be refused entry, but he waved me through.

I was allowed upstairs and shown into an office. Two walls were covered by audio equipment, banks of tape machines, and other mysterious technical *matériel*, dials, lights and switches. It looked like a set designer's idea of the heart of a network designed to take over the world. The forensic detective was clean-cut and tall, with something of the 'short back and sides' of the military man. As he made us coffee, he filled me in on his background. He told me that he had spent sixteen years as an electronics engineer in the Royal Navy, which explained his brisk manner, mostly in submarines listening in to various atmospheric conversations, echoes of secrets being passed from potential enemy to enemy. Then he had joined the Metropolitan Police where his skills at computing and electronic eavesdropping had led him to the top of the Forensic Audio Laboratory, which was just coming into its own at the time. He had been called upon to assist with frontline work on authentication and enhancement at several terrorist trials, work that involved providing urgent answers on legal cases in response to lawyers' demands and then defending his findings before an aggressive barrister. From there he had set up his own company in the commercial sector, although his main client remained the police service, which probably explained the security guard's question. The company undertook forensics work, computer retrieval, information technology, video and audio enhancement, analysis and transcription of video and audio tapes, and had recently developed a

3D crime scene modelling unit. Although the detective himself specialized in audio rather than documentary evidence, he was knowledgeable about the use of equipment to analyse paper and writing. He had agreed to see me – and the letter – out of pure intellectual curiosity which, given the state of my finances, was more than helpful. 'If necessary,' he said, 'we can get one of the specialists in.'

Before I unpacked the bottle, he told me he would show me his favourite toys. I was impressed by his discipline and refusal to look at the letter until he had explained things to our mutual satisfaction. First he showed me an ACO tester. It looked a little like a computer screen, but hollowed out, like a hood, which shone light on the document beneath it. The detective explained that ACO was just the trade name, that the equipment was a form of vectoral comparator, but more compact. It felt more and more like a scene from a James Bond film, with the detective in the role of Q.

'It is capable of looking at indentations on paper,' the forensic detective continued, 'but it is generally used to look at inks. The idea is that each individual ink will fluoresce at a different light, even though the manufacturer may be the same, so when you've got two black inks, they will fluoresce at slightly different wavelengths.' He slid a test card, a bogus cheque from 'Nicky Smith', under the hood to demonstrate what he meant. Then he adjusted the type of light and the frequency, did something to the filter and twiddled the focus button until the inks began to separate out. It became clear that Ms Smith had written a cheque for £6 and some fraudster had increased it to £60, but though the forgery was indistinguishable to the naked eye, it was clear under the ACO tester.

Then he turned to the piece of equipment that resembled a small fax machine with a glass hood over the top of it. This was the ESDA machine. I had done my homework and knew this was the contraption that had brought down the West Midlands Serious Crime Squad and had exposed a string of other miscarriages of justice when a Birmingham University academic, Tom Davis, had used it to prove that the police had forged confessions. Davis then worked on the murder of PC Blakelock in the Broadwater Farm riots of 1985 and the Birmingham pub bombings of 1974, two of the highest-profile cases of the time. 'ESDA is an extraordinary machine,' he had written. 'It brings to light evidence that was not only hitherto completely invisible, but whose very existence was unknown.' When I had first heard of this procedure from the private detective, I had joked that in a perfect world the letter-writer would have written her name and address on the page above in the pad.

'There's a vacuum pump in the bottom of the equipment that draws the document down through tiny holes and flattens it on to a bed,' the forensic detective explained. 'If we cover that document in plastic to protect it, we can charge the document up using a probe with 5,000 volts of static electricity. Now any of the paper nap that has been indented will lift up. So even though physically you can't see anything on the paper, written in ink, something's been indented into it. Then we spray the document over the top of the plastic with carbon granules and these adhere themselves to the indentations on the document, should there be any. And then, if we're very clever, we can lift the plastic off and put it over a white piece of paper, and then Xerox it, so you've got a record of the indentations.' Wonderful.

'To do that,' the detective continued, 'we do need to humidify the document. It's a very simple process; you have to leave the document in a tray that has water in it, just so that it dampens the paper itself. This lets the electrostatic electricity get hold of the nap of the paper.'

This seemed to me one of my most promising avenues of research – and the detective was infected by my optimism. He was ready to begin. He put on rubber medical gloves and began to slide the letter out of the bottle. I appreciated the little professional touch of the gloves. I noticed that his fingers were trembling slightly and was gratified to see that even a forensic detective was excited by the possibility of cracking the mystery.

The first problem was that the letter was rolled into such a tight scroll only a centimetre or so in diameter. The detective unrolled it, and then unfolded the pages. 'These large creases could cause a problem for the ESDA machine,' he commented worriedly, as he struggled to flatten the pages.

It got worse. 'It's been written on both sides. This is a problem for the ESDA machine because one side is imprinted on the other.'

I could feel my optimism evaporating. I pointed out that the third sheet of the letter had nothing written on the back, but by then the detective had discovered the final obstacle. 'This paper is sort of plastic-coated, and we will have to be very careful with that. The ink hasn't penetrated the paper very much. It's just stayed on top and dried, not permeated in, so we'll be very lucky to find anything.'

I showed him the smudge the graphologist had made. She had wanted to check whether the letter was written with a rollerball-type pen, and before I could stop her, she had licked her finger and wiped it over a word. The ink had followed her finger across the paper in a little blue smudge.

'Yes, this is worrying me,' said the detective. 'As soon as it touches anything damp, that ink's going to run. If we put it into the humidifier tray, with this ink and this paper, we're going to create a lot of damage. The ink's going to just slide off the paper. That will be the end of everything.'

I felt terribly protective towards the letter. When the graphologist had smudged the word, I had been annoyed; it had caused me something like a physical jolt, an irritation unconnected to the fact that she was possibly polluting the document by adding her DNA along with her saliva to it. I was not going to risk putting the letter in a tray of liquid and being left with a white sheet and a bowl of blue water. And somehow, the fact that the letter was holding on to its mysteries once again confirmed its status, even in the eyes of this clever professional with his serried banks of technical equipment.

We decided to check the letter on the ACO tester anyhow, since that caused no permanent physical damage. The detective placed the flattened sheets one by one under the filter and twiddled the dials until the ink disappeared from the paper and he was left with anything else there might be. 'There's a crossing out, a bit of white-out.' He confirmed the graphologist's comment that the letter-writer had used a line guide, for every line was exactly on top of the one on the reverse side of the sheet. There were no other indentations on the sheet, so he assured me that the ESDA would not have yielded any more information even if we had been able to use it. It seemed plausible because any indentations would surely have been revealed under the fluorescent light too. He agreed that the pages were pulled from a pad, that there were little roundels at the top of the sheet, where the page had been torn off, and that the page had probably been ripped from left to right.

'That narrows it down,' he proclaimed, clearly trying to console me after the failure of the ESDA machine.

'What, to people owning a pad?'

'Yes,' he nodded. 'Maybe sixty billion?'

'And francophone and female,' I reminded him. We smiled. 'Why, I'm nearly there.'

My next move was to ring a specialist ribbon shop, renowned through-out the world. The locks of hair had been tied together with a narrow pale-blue ribbon. The shop I chose was based in London so at least the conversation could be carried out in my mother tongue, although I hung up with the feeling that I had failed to make myself properly understood. But I did manage to establish that they would definitely know all about the ribbon; even though they would never reveal their manufacturing sources, they might be able to supply some useful information. I doubted this, given how the research was going, but if you're clutching at straws, a ribbon was a satisfactory alternative.

The shop was situated in one of London's most exclusive neighbour-hoods. A little treasure trove of colourful trimmings, ties and decorations, it was packed with ribbon browsers. As soon as I showed the manager the tiny light-blue strip of material he knew the answer with barely a glance. 'Berisford,' he said. 'Manufactured in France. Sold throughout the country.' He gave it another look. 'The colour is called Sky, 10mm. Used for christenings, dinner-table settings.'

So there would be no way to track down who had bought it, or rather who had sold it? I persisted. No. Silly question, of course.

By now, the other clients had paused in their perusal of the goods and the shop had fallen very quiet. Some people looked round; others just showed by the set of their shoulders and the stillness of their hands that they were eavesdropping with intent.

I was rather pleased with myself for having discovered the name of the ribbon manufacturer. It turned out that Berisfords was in fact founded in Congleton in Cheshire in 1858 by three brothers, Charles, William and Francis. Congleton was noted as a centre for silk throwing and weaving as early as the 1750s. Purchase by a Swiss company in 1992 had enabled the development of 'a more European look to its ribbons'. The ribbon investigation was turning into research for research's sake but I did manage to ascertain that there were numerous French outlets. Perhaps there had been a faint chance that the ribbon was so special that it might have provided some clues, but the straw had turned out, when grasped, to be just that: a straw.

The only other physical element that I had not yet investigated was the pot-pourri of sandalwood shavings in the bottle, but surely that was beyond the call of obsession. It didn't need a superior shopkeeper to tell me that any analysis of the pot-pourri was time wasted. By now I was beginning to feel very depressed about the whole quest, and starting to wonder whether it was a displacement activity for something missing in my own life. Perhaps I needed to get a job – on a supermarket check-out even – to take my mind off this unsolved mystery.

18

One day a friend brought me a present. 'I saw it and thought of your search and couldn't resist it,' she said.

Beautifully wrapped, it turned out to be a message-in-a-bottle kit. A nice little box covered in cliché pictures: desert island, frolicking dolphins, three-mast sailing ship, seagull, whale, starfish. Inside sat a glass bottle with a cork stopper, a small bag of red sealing wax and a tea-light. The message was already written – all that was left was to fill in the gaps:

> Ahoy,
> Be it known that [. . . name]
> set this adrift on [. . . date].
> I live at [. . . location].

And, in a picture of a lifebelt, there was a little space for a photograph. Couldn't be made any easier really. I was very touched that she had thought of me.

Just as I was tucking the sealing wax back under the bottle and closing the lid of the kit, I caught sight of a red helicopter hovering outside my study window, clearly seeking somewhere to land. Then it veered off and landed a few hundred metres up the road, on a patch of open ground. Police cordoned off my street, and when I asked an officer what had happened, he said that a young lad coming home from school had been hit at the zebra crossing and the helicopter was taking him to hospital. That day my own son was travelling home from school on his own for the first time, using the bus and train. He had tried the previous two days, but the buses had failed to stop on his request, and after an hour and a half, as darkness set in, I had gone to collect him. Today was to be his third effort, and if the bus ignored him again he was determined to walk to the train station. I quickly calculated where he would be – not out of school yet – and my daughter also still at school for a play rehearsal. Then I thought of Maurice and my heart went out to this child and his mother. Just because you're paranoid doesn't mean your child is not in danger. Life is fragile and I felt a renewed sympathy for the mother and her loss.

In between trying to find the letter-writer and the interminable, boring minutiae of motherhood – the precious neurons dedicated to remembering what stage of the laundry cycle the rugby gear has reached, or where a history essay has been secreted, the constant juggling of domestic and school needs, the trips, events, homework, social life of children – I walked the dog, and thanked my fate for the precious trivia.

In the park I met a woman who was sad because she had sent her child away to boarding school. 'I'm sure I'll get used to it,' she told me, though in her eyes there was the panic of empty days that had previously been filled with school runs and tea parties and tennis lessons and the weekly family shop and the nightly dinner to cook.

Better the dullness of routine and the security of being needed. Better that than the creaking absence of a part of oneself.

I was now beginning to attract sympathetic yawns from my friends when I said I had a few remaining leads to follow up ('Found her yet? What, not *still* looking, are you?'). But I continued to feel that I had not explored all the potential clues that the bottle might hold. Surely there must be some kind of recall code somewhere on the bottle, some way for Evian to trace their product if there were ever to be a problem. Once more I rang my contact at Evian headquarters. She was reluctant to reopen a subject that she considered she had covered in depth, especially since she had been the one to suggest a link between the letter and the *Message in a Bottle* film. She was also very busy and it took me several weeks to catch her between marketing trips to China and Peru. Initially, however, she continued to deny that there might ever be a problem requiring the factory to track their bottles.

'But if there were a glass splinter or something . . .' I began, but she cut in. Clearly the possibility of glass splinters was not going down well on the public relations front. I tried again. 'Look, there is a number 46 on the base, and down the side of the bottle, parallel to the seam along the glass, it says 3 06832 0011516. Why don't I fly over and show you?'

'I won't be here. There is nothing further to discover from the bottle – it would be a complete waste of your time,' she replied firmly. 'Wait, I'll go and get my bottle.'

A few moments later she returned to the phone. 'What was the number?' I repeated it. 'No, that's just the bar code, my bottle has exactly the same number.'

'There must be some way . . .' I couldn't bear to hang up after finally getting hold of her. 'Normally there is a sort of plastic label around the neck,' she offered. 'But I don't suppose that it is still there?'

'No,' I replied sadly. 'And inside the lid of the bottle it just says PP. What's PP?'

'Polypropylene.' I could hear the *tsk* at my stupidity. 'And the code on the metal lid only tells you when it was bottled.'

'What metal lid?'

'Well, for instance on my lid, I can tell you that this water was bottled at 16.15 on the . . .'

'Mine hasn't got a metal lid, just some white tape and sticky stuff.'

Impatiently and with the deliberate clarity of one talking to a foreigner or a less intelligent person, she talked me through: 'First you have a blue plastic pointed cap . . . take it off . . . then underneath is the metal lid . . . well, on the side of that top is the factory code and production details.'

'Yes, I understand that. It's just that this bottle no longer has a metal lid.'

'Well, there you go.' Invisible but conclusive shrug. 'Even if you had it, you could only track the water back to the factory, not onwards to the point of sale. But anyhow, you don't have the lid, so there's absolutely no point in your flying over to see us.'

The thought of the eccentric Englishwoman showing up on Evian's doorstep had concentrated her mind very effectively. Just as I had a mental image of her in a Chanel suit, immaculately coiffed and manicured, so she must have a picture of me, some obsessed mad person rabbiting on about beach flotsam.

After she had hung up, I stared at the bottle for a while. So how had the letter-writer sealed it so effectively just with tape to make it waterproof? I decided to try and pick away the white sticky tape that had formed the seal. And suddenly I caught a glimpse of something blue beneath the glue. With all the excitement of a treasure hunter I picked away more scabs of adhesive and then chiselled out the encrusted lid. I could feel my heart beat faster, and wondered at my own reaction to such a minute discovery.

```
From: Karen Liebreich
To Director of External Relations, Danone
Subject: Letter in a Bottle


Dear [Mme Evian],
Please excuse me for continuing to pester you about
this letter in the bottle. After we spoke last week,
I was rather disappointed. But then I had another
closer look at the bottle, and began to pick off the
tape and glue, and in fact the top is there,
although quite damaged by the glue and by my efforts
to ease it out from the plastic lid where it had got
wedged.
    The code on the lid is: 297 19:34.
    What does that mean?
```

I know you are away travelling, and these
requests for information must be rather irritating,
but I feel I must follow this trail right to the
end.

Thank you very much for your help,

Regards,

Karen

From: [Mme Evian]

To: Karen Liebreich

Subject: Letter in a Bottle

Herewith some answers to your queries, but I CAN DO
NO MORE:

Here are the details about the production of this
bottle:

- This Millennium 2002 bottle was produced on
  24 October 2001.
- It comes from a 'box' production, in other words a
  presentation stand for large areas intended for the
  metro.
- During that day, 24 October 2001, we produced 130
  boxes, in other words 60,840 bottles.

- During the week of 22–26 October 2001 we produced
  649 boxes, in other words 303,732 bottles.

  But you must consider that an English citizen
  could buy this bottle in France and return to
  England with it . . . so you really are hunting for
  a needle in a haystack.

  For us the matter is now *completely terminated*.
  Regards.

I had not been wrong about the Evian lady's feelings towards me. She had been helpful, she had done her duty, she had answered the madwoman's questions. Our relationship was now *completely terminated*. But she had provided more clues. Just when I was about to give up the trail, I was back in business.

So the letter-writer was likely to be a Parisian, since the bottles were 'intended for the metro'. As she was rushing back from work one day, through the crowded tunnels, the unknown mother was stopped in her tracks by the sight of a water dispenser filled with beautiful tear-shaped bottles. They seemed to beckon to her, and speak through the grime of urban travel about distant waves and sea spray. She scrabbled desperately in her bag for some coins. She would use the bottle to send a message . . .

But . . . Before I leapt to conclusions – maybe there were metros in other large French towns? If the factory knows exactly when the bottle was produced, why can't they track down exactly to which metro it went? But the Evian lady was so clearly fed up with the whole subject and with me that I dared not write again. Instead I sent out a desperate query email to five French friends.

My friends started to reply:

```
Are you sure she said 'LA metro'? If she did, that
means metropolitan France, in other words it was not
intended for export or for anywhere beyond the main-
land.
```

A short while later a second friend replied:

```
Bad luck, there are metros throughout France.
```

A friend whose husband is a French historian specializing in the First World War was the third to answer my email. Her husband's books deal with the historic relationships between mothers and their children: grieving mothers whose sons were killed on the battlefields, children in battle and the conflict between maternal affection and the revulsion that raped women feel towards the resulting offspring. This friend wrote:

Sadly there are many Metros. Check out their website.

I followed the hypertext link she had included on her email to discover that Metro is the fifth largest world distribution group, with Walmart in first place. Metro runs Cash & Carry-type stores across northern France. The largest – 16,000 square metres – is at Lomme/Lille, the next at Rouen. Along the coast itself there are two stores, at Caën and at Calais. This was a whole new – and unwelcome – linguistic development.

'How do you know it is not the underground kind of metro?' I queried. The reply was firm: '"Grandes surfaces" [large areas] in Evian's email means supermarkets,' she wrote. 'And there is no capital letter on Metro, because I think it is a diminutive of "la société métro" – the metro company, and perhaps that is also why it is used in the feminine.'

The image of the letter-writer stopping to buy a bottle of water in the crowded Paris underground and suddenly being overwhelmed by the urge to write a letter in a bottle evaporated.

I spoke to the distribution manager for Metro Calais, a huge warehouse depot on the outskirts of the city. I explained that Evian had sent out a consignment of Millennium bottles some time shortly after 24 October 2001 and asked whether there was any way of tracking to which Metro store they would have been dispatched. If I had the receipt for the bottle, he said, he could tell me. If I had the receipt for the bottle, I felt like snapping, I would not need to talk to you now. The store and its address would presumably be written on the receipt.

But he was friendly, so I told him the story so far, and he was helpful in the same kind of discouraging way as nearly everyone else whose interest had been caught by it. He assured me that given his knowledge of the Channel currents – acquired at the back of the warehouse, unloading supermarket deliveries – it was likely to have been his store that sold the bottle.

In a curious fashion I was again beginning to enjoy the letter-in-a-bottle quest. The story I told each new person had an emotional kick, and although I often sighed inwardly as I began to recount the tale again, I was not yet tired of telling of the distraught mother and her dead son, and of my efforts to track her down. For the first time the thought occurred to me that it was a way of making new acquaintances. How else would I have had the chance to meet secret policemen, warehouse distributors, high-flying public relations executives, private investigators, forensic detectives? Perhaps this whole quest was simply a way of filling a lonely day while the children were at school and my partner at work? Or a way of embarking on a study of human nature by private correspondence, rather than by signing up for a course at evening school. It was certainly true that I was learning a great deal about a variety of esoteric subjects, but perhaps I was also learning more about myself. I had been shocked at the speed and shallowness of my powers of logic, and slightly worried by the obsessive nature of my desire to find the mother. I had been forced to touch on the idea of death and had seen how unwilling my mind was to confront its possibility in direct relation to myself or to those I loved.

I had also realized the limitations of my French. Metro proved to be yet another red herring. Whether the supermarket chain or the underground system, it carried me no further forward. The time had come to publicize my search, to follow the advice of the follicologist and the private investigator. I decided to put my toe in the water gradually.

19

I rang *La Voix du Nord*, the regional newspaper for northern France, whose death columns I had so fruitlessly perused months earlier, and explained that I wanted to place an advert. The lady in charge of small ads asked me which section I wished to advertise in and was utterly bemused when I explained the subject matter – she had no idea which section would be appropriate. Would I like to speak to editorial? I jumped at the chance. The editor was interested and asked for a photograph of me and the bottle on the beach. I ran to my neighbour and press-ganged her son to rush down to the banks of the Thames with me and his camera. His brief was simple: Make this muddy riverine beach at low tide look like the sea at Warden Bay on the Isle of Sheppey; make me look tall, blonde and irresistibly attractive, and make this bottle look mysteriously intriguing.

It was an impossible task, but the bottle looked fine in the photograph, so I posted it off with a short explanation to the editor at *La Voix du Nord*.

Encouraged by this reception I decided to cast my net wider. I placed a small ad in *Libération*, the left-of-centre French national daily. The lady in the sales department announced that the category was no problem – 'Between ourselves: seeking' – but the text I had written, she said, was useless. She spent twenty minutes reworking the information with me, only to inform me that the advert was now twelve lines long and would cost me a fortune. We spent another five minutes trimming it back to a more affordable size. It now read:

"SAUVE" 01.45.88.95.63

vie pratique

RECHERCHE

Trouvé une bouteille à la mer...
Maurice décédé à 13 ans.
Qui est sa maman ?
bouteillealamere@hotmail.com

OBJETS PERDUS

SOS : Aidez-moi.
Montre-pendentif avec chaîne,
perdue le 21/04/04, à Paris M° 8,

Found

A letter in a bottle . . .

Maurice died aged 13 years

Who is his mother?

bouteillealamere@hotmail.com

As she took my credit card details she expressed the hope that the advert would be effective, and remarked sadly that she would never know the result. When I offered to ring her if it worked, she gratefully offered me an extra free insertion.

Libération – two insertions had been and gone, with no result. For some reason my advert was placed under the subsection 'Practical Life' in the 'Between Ourselves' section, and mine was the only one in it. I think I would have preferred the subsection 'Personal Messages'. Then I could have been next to: 'I am happy to be immortal, so that I could love you for eternity. Why have you abandoned me?' and 'Yes, that's right. See you soon I hope.'

When there was only one Saturday small ad left between myself and despair I checked my Hotmail account and realized there was a message waiting. It was the first message that had not been from the staff at Hotmail. This could be an important lead, I said to myself. My heart became arrhythmic and my chest tightened.

> Bonjour, please excuse me, I saw your small ad in
> Libé. I would like to do a report on found bottles.
> However, I don't have enough information, which is
> why I am writing to you. Please give me more
> information.
>   Many thanks in advance.

My heartbeat returned to normal.

Every time I opened my email account, I felt the same tension. But every day there was nothing. I rang *La Voix du Nord* and asked them if they had received the photographs of me and the bottle with the River Thames standing in for the sea. They finally decided to run the article. Nowhere in London could I find a copy of *La Voix du Nord*. I had no idea what they had written.

In the final insertion for the small ad in *Libération*, mine was one of five in its section, which provided an eclectic mixture of requests: for lodgings, for help with translation from Swedish, suggestions for a future career for an ex-pro footballer, and blunt demands for money with which to make a new life.

The editor at *La Voix du Nord* had promised to send me a copy. Meanwhile I opened my resolutely empty e-mail inbox ten times a day. I realized that it was not enough to have advertised in only one national paper and to have had a single article in the main local press for northern France. Convinced that I had to make a more comprehensive effort to publicize my quest, I rang *Le Figaro*. Once again the lady at the switchboard needed to know exactly which category of small ad I was seeking to place. 'The one where you look for a person who sent a letter in a bottle,' I explained wearily. The novelty value of explaining to intermediaries had worn off. 'I'll put you through to editorial,' she said after only a moment's thought.

Once again I explained to the person in editorial that I had been trying to place a small ad, but that the receptionist thought editorial might be interested.

'We don't do bottles,' she interrupted me.

This was a new departure. 'Could you explain why?' I enquired, intrigued.

'We just don't do bottles.'

'Is there a reason for this policy decision?'

'We never do them.'

By now I was annoyed – I hadn't asked to be put through to editorial, but since I had, I was not going to be put off so easily. I asked to speak to her boss, and she reluctantly complied. I explained my requirements once more. The boss partially covered her handpiece and called the elements of the story over the office to the editor . . . 'There's a woman here who found a bottle, with a letter, in England – are you interested?' 'Yes, can we have the details?' 'A journalist will be calling you . . .'

Over the next few weeks I tried once or twice more to place an advert and was always put on hold for the editorial department who never called back. Whoever thought it would be so hard to spend money advertising for information?

The published article in *La Voix du Nord* finally arrived in the post, several weeks after it had appeared. It was satisfyingly large, carried the photograph and a plaintive article beneath, and my email address, correctly spelt, at the bottom. It had attracted absolutely no response – neither to me nor to the newspaper.

When, after blocking my frequent attempts at advertising, *Le Figaro* failed to act on its initial interest, I decided to try another medium. I emailed the main Calais radio station, in what I thought was a suitably upbeat, casual manner:

```
Hello, I am writing to you from London. I found a
bottle on an English beach with a letter in French
```

Appel

Une bouteille à la mer retrouvée dans le Kent

Qui est l'auteur du message ?

Anonyme, le message qui se trouvait dans la bouteille est « triste et émouvant », raconte Karen Liebreich.

On pourrait croire que cela n'arrive que dans les romans ou dans les films. Mais non. Une Anglaise a bel et bien retrouvé une bouteille jetée à la mer et porteuse d'un message, sur une plage du Kent. La trouvaille n'est pas nouvelle. Elle remonte à février 2002.

Elle s'est d'abord renseignée sur les courants marins pour essayer d'identifier la provenance de la bouteille. « *Elle vient de la Manche* », informe-t-elle. Elle a ensuite fait des recherches à la Bibliothèque nationale à Paris, recherchant dans les collections de *La Voix du Nord* ᵕᵃᵉ ᵈⁿ ᵈᵉᶜᵉʳ ⁴ˡ⁻ ⁱ᷊᷉ˀ⁻

in it. Who is Maurice, died aged thirteen? The letter haunts me. Can you ask your listeners for information?

I followed up on the telephone and initially the producer seemed very interested. However, an urgent deadline was always looming, and after being fobbed off a few times, my enthusiasm waned.

I knew I was reaching the end of the road. Stopping now felt like mislaying a gripping thriller thirty pages from the end, just before discovering whodunnit. But I had no choice. I had no idea how to get on French television and it seemed there was no other way of finding the letter-writer. My friend the dog-walker rang for a chat and asked me how the search was going. I told her it was over. I had done everything I could. I had spent time, money and energy talking to endless statisticians, detectives, journalists, an astrologer and a tarot reader. I had got it out of my system, the scab had been picked, now I was going to try and leave it to heal. I was irritable. I almost blamed my friend for having shown me the letter in the first place. 'It was an awful letter,' she said. 'I only read it twice. It upset me so much I had to put it away. I've never looked at it since.'

As I put the telephone down I realized that the unknown mother and her grief had almost faded away in the excitement – and more recently the boredom – of the chase. In the excitement of meeting detectives and astrologers, of hunting through archives, and chasing round ribbon shops, I had somewhere let slip the essential tragedy.

That evening I read the letter again and I wept again. The next morning, with a final burst of renewed determination, I went back through all the notes I had kept as I talked to people on the telephone. There were still a couple of loose ends . . . I would just follow those up, I thought. One last police contact and one final 'New Age' lead. And then I would be free.

One of my French friends had mentioned a friend who was a police superintendent in Rouen. After the bad experience with the secret police chief in Paris who had promised so much and achieved nothing, I was not expecting a warm welcome. But I got one. His friend had prepared him and he had been waiting for me to call. On the telephone I explained the background and awaited his analysis. It came by email within the hour:

```
I think we could be dealing with an adolescent
suicide. It's not a certainty, but an impression
given by the expressions used by the mother.
```

He made other suggestions, all of which I had already followed up. He also strongly denied that there was any secret national database, as the police chief had hinted, that would collect all the births, deaths and marriages held by the town halls. He could offer no concrete assistance, only his opinion. It seemed that there really was no clever computer search engine that could reveal the death of Maurice by typing in 'Maurice, aged thirteen'. It had turned out to be a figment of my wishful imagination, encouraged into existence by the unreliable secret policeman.

The last uncontacted number in my notes was that of a radiesthesist, a pendulum swinger. The tarot reader I had consulted months ago had seen one, and this had triggered her search for her own mother – the search that the tarot reader had spent two decades completing. The pendulum had directed her to a small village in south-west France, and had reassured her that her mother was indeed still alive and would welcome a call. The geography and the welcome had apparently both been accurately predicted by the pendulum.

Pendulum swinging, radiesthesy, dowsing using a moving pendulum, is carried out by a person with an unusual sensitivity using a rod or pendulum to amplify the message. Usually the pendulum is a small ball attached to a thin string on the end of a stick. The string is made of a non-woven material, such as nylon, so that no extraneous forces are introduced. The swinger must also be very careful not to allow any of his own movements or muscle-twitching to influence the activity of the pendulum. It can be used to locate missing objects, and for medical diagnosis. The term *radiesthésie* was coined in 1930 by Abbé

Bouly in France when the pendulum took preference over the rod as the instrument of choice. L'Association des amis de la radiesthésie was established in 1930 and the British Society of Dowsers three years later.

When asked a question, a clockwise rotation is a yes, an anti-clockwise one a no. A more sophisticated version is teleradiesthesia or superpendulism, when the sensitive person is presented with a map. 'After placing the pendulum on the map,' says an informative website, 'he can tell the enquirer the information he wants to know.' The pendulum seemed to be my last resort.

But I was due for a disappointment. The radiesthesist had quit. She had become unsure of her own skill, although still convinced of the value of the pendulum, and had decided to hang up her bob and string and rod, and lead a quiet life of retirement. After the antici-pation, I couldn't face seeking a replacement. She had come highly recommended by the tarot reader, and I tried to convince her to take on one last case. She held firm, but when I persisted she made another suggestion.

She recommended that I consult a clairvoyant in Paris – 'the best in France' – and gave me the details. 'This number is not available to the general public, you are very privileged to get it,' she told me.

20

The clairvoyant's website spoke of visions facilitated by crystal balls covered in wisps of black muslin, but as I read on my shiver of apprehension was tempered by the usual rush of scepticism. She was 'France's most famous clairvoyant', with a long list of celebrities and minor royal figures as clients. Every night she was invited to 'parties, dinners, openings, events'. According to the website Mme Clairvoyant had a waiting list six months' long but I booked an appointment in a few weeks' time, and made my travel arrangements.

The clairvoyant lived in an impressive apartment block near the Boulevard St-Germain, on the Left Bank. Looking up from the pavement, I could see wisteria straddling the gaps along the fourth-floor balconies, running the length of the building. The usual massive

communal doors of Parisian apartments led into a mirrored hallway, with a rank of high-powered all-terrain pushchairs parked under the last loop of the staircase. The secretary on the intercom murmured 'fourth floor' and I squeezed into a tiny lift that had been cunningly inserted into the stairwell, as nineteenth-century grandeur was sacrificed to convenience. Even alone I felt my personal space was being infringed, although the maximum possible weight was apparently three people. As I emerged from the lift and took a few deep breaths to prepare myself, I bumped into the concierge who was distributing the mail to the apartments.

The door was immediately opened by an elegant, beautifully clad lady in pressed white linen trousers and shirt, who held out her hand in welcome. As I shook her hand and tried to step through the half-open door, my foot tripped on the mat in the hallway, under which the concierge had left the post, including letters and packages. It was not the entry I had planned, but I warmed to the lady as she swooped gracefully down to extricate her mail with some aplomb.

She showed me into her office and disappeared for a few moments, leaving me to organize my thoughts and look around. The apartment was large and high-ceilinged, but crammed with works of art, paintings, sculptures and ornaments, predominantly in the Louis XV style. Behind the desk hung an enormous nineteenth-century portrait of a beautiful woman in a pink dress clasping a posy. Every inch of the walls was covered with paintings, including works signed by Toulouse-Lautrec and other famous artists. In the corner of the room stood a small clavichord. Lying on coffee tables were art books and magazines. Interspersed among the bookshelves were portraits of a handsome young man, clearly the son of the clairvoyant.

I was worried that my scepticism, engendered by the celebrity endorsements on her website, would be immediately apparent and I would be shown the (magnificently rococo) door. But the lady settled herself at the desk, her dark hair becomingly drawn back in a chignon, one impressive ring on her hand, and looked at me in a warm and approachable manner. Her secretary had encouraged me to 'bring photos of your loved ones, anything you like to show Madame'. I had brought just the bottle with its contents.

I unpacked it and set it on the table before the clairvoyant.

The clairvoyant leaned forward in the chair. I felt curious and cynical. 'What's this?' she asked.

'A letter in a bottle. I would like you to tell me about it.'

Her brows lifted in interest. I had not mentioned the letter in a bottle on the phone, and it was unlikely that she would have known anything about it. If she had looked me up on the internet she would not have found any link to letters in bottles. It was not that I wanted to test her, it was more that I wanted her to come to the subject free of preconceptions and uninfluenced by my previous investigations.

'Can I open it and read the letter?' she asked.

'I'd prefer you to tell me what you can before reading the letter,' I answered firmly.

She nodded, unperturbed. 'First I'll see if I can pick up your signal or not. I'll tell you whether I can feel anything.' She handed me a pack of picture cards. 'Shuffle these well,' she instructed me.

They were not tarot cards, but various crudely drawn pictures, well thumbed and patched up with Sellotape around the edges. When I queried what they were, she explained, 'They are my own special

221

cards. They are just an aid to clairvoyance, my way of working. The cards help me. I don't believe in them as such, it simply helps one to get in the mood, to make a connection with you, then afterwards it's clairvoyance. If you don't have the sight, these cards are completely useless.'

I was a bit disappointed, having promised myself crystal balls and dark muslin. I tried to concentrate as instructed, cut the pack and passed it to her.

'Is there a death in connection with this person?' she asked immediately. 'I see death. I see death, something very hard, something like a cry for help . . . Perhaps it is a cry for help. There is something terribly unpleasant here, which is giving me a headache, something very painful.'

Her brow creased in concentration and – perhaps – pain.

'There is something very upsetting in your story, something painful, difficult. This bottle is giving me a real feeling of physical discomfort. It is linked to a death. I feel very unwell . . . I feel very uneasy.'

I tried to keep my expression inscrutable, not to give her any unnecessary leads, but I was impressed. A letter in a bottle is not usually linked to death. After all, 75 per cent of the 435 messages in the bottles which Wim Kruiswijk collected over his two-decade sample analysis were simply looking for a penfriend – and of the rest not one was classified as containing subject matter relating to death.

'Is it a woman who wrote? Because I can see a woman.' I nodded. 'I see a woman suffering. I feel dreadful. I have a terrible headache beginning, a very violent headache.'

I must say she didn't look particularly ill. But her manner was not melodramatic, she seemed to be simply telling me how she felt. She shuffled her cards again.

'Give me thirteen cards,' she ordered. 'I have a terrible headache, you have no idea how it feels.'

She laid out the cards on the desk. 'Yes, there is something very difficult, something painful here, there is a death in connection with this. I sense violence. I see a woman with mid-length hair, quite long hair . . .' She swept her hands down the side of her face to indicate hair falling straight down to just below the shoulders. 'Loose, like this,' the imaginary hair flowed past her own neat chignon.

'There is something very troubling,' she continued, fingering the battered cards. 'I see a woman with longish hair, quite thin, slim, I see someone – it's very strange, how can I explain it to you? I think the person who threw this in did it quite deliberately, but I feel that something is not quite right in that person's mind. I think the woman is quite . . . "deranged" is not the right word . . . I'd say "perturbed" rather.'

So far, she seemed spot-on, but I was careful to give her no encouragement,

'Does she speak of the death of a man?' she went on. 'I see a death of someone male.'

'Yes,' I said. 'A boy.'

'Yes, there is a death of someone male.'

'How do you know?' I asked, peering at the pictures on her cards. There was nothing simple and obvious – like the tarot card for Death – to indicate this.

'Because I see it,' she replied simply. 'The death is linked to the violence of a man,' she hesitated, and moved the cards around. 'Yes, that death of the child is linked to the violence of a man. The child is – what – ten to fifteen years old, twelve years old?'

'Thirteen.'

She nodded. 'I think this death is linked to the violence of a man, amongst other things . . .' She tailed off, then repeated, 'Violence by a man.'

There was a pause. I wondered fancifully whether the child had been conceived during a rape, since no man was mentioned in the letter, nor was there any reference to a man in connection with the lives of the mother or child, or the boy's death.

'Where did you find it, on an English coast?'

I nodded.

'Does it come from a boat?'

This time I shrugged.

'I think it comes from a boat,' she answered herself. 'I think it definitely comes from a boat. I see a woman clearly, I ask myself whether it comes from a woman who is on a boat . . . There is some violence. Does she speak of violence in the letter? Or of difficult things?'

'Well, yes, the death, that's difficult,' I answered unhelpfully.

'Is the letter written in French?' she interrupted.

'Yes.' I was deliberately trying to provide bald uninformative statements.

'Yes, I see French writing, it comes from someone French . . .' Not difficult, I had just told her that. 'I see a sailing boat, a kind of half sailing, half motor boat, not very big . . .' Not a cross-Channel ferry then. 'I see this woman, I see this death, I see violence on the boat, the cries of violence . . . It's strange, I see someone diving, trying to get something, but they can't reach it. As though they are trying to recover something from underwater.'

'Give me another card.' She glared at the picture I had handed her. 'It's not easy . . . give me another card . . . It's not someone old who did this. Someone of about forty, more or less . . . fortyish, maybe fifty. Another card. Another . . . Does she speak of violence with a man? Something difficult with a man?'

'The death of her son,' I answered, and then was annoyed with myself. I had given her an unnecessary clue, the precise relationship of the dead boy. We were fencing.

She nodded, as though it were no surprise. 'May I touch the letter now?' she asked.

As she opened the bottle and tipped out the letter she continued to ask questions. 'How long ago did you find it?'

'February . . .' I began and hesitated as I wrestled to convert the year into French.

'One, two years ago?' she asked.

Meanwhile she was opening up the bottle, unfolding the letter. The lock of hair fell out. 'Is this the child's hair?' she asked. 'At all events, the mother has hair like this. Exactly like this.'

I told her there were two separate locks intertwined.

'Anyhow this is the mother's hair,' she repeated. 'That's exactly the right colour.'

Another occasion missed when I could have proven her findings – I should have asked her to specify the hair colour before she saw the hair.

She spread the letter out on her desk. 'The writing is from someone very disturbed,' she repeated. She shook her head. 'Before reading it, I would say it's the writing of someone really disturbed. One would say someone who wants to die.'

She glanced at the first sheet. 'It's very long,' she commented, discouraged by the density of the writing and the number of pages. 'Why don't you summarize it for me.'

'Well,' I began. 'Her son died, at the dawn of summer . . .'

'I have such a terrible headache when I hold this letter,' the clairvoyant interrupted me. 'There is a madness in this woman. Does the letter seem coherent to you?'

'Given that she has lost her son . . .' I prevaricated.

'Yes, I see what you mean. Go on,' she encouraged me.

I skimmed through some of the more striking phrases. 'My life started when he was born . . . he slipped away from life . . . Forgive me for being so angry at your disappearance . . . I think there's been some mistake . . .' I told her about the last line, that the mother would show the letter only to one friend.

'My impression is of a woman who is losing her reason.' She broke off again: 'I have such an incredibly violent pain in the head. I have to put the letter away.'

She began to cram it back into the bottle desperately. Others – the graphologist, my friend the dog-walker, the forensic detective, myself – treated the letter more like a holy relic, an important piece of precious evidence, rolling up the sheets immaculately. The clairvoyant was in a hurry to get rid of it. Like a genie, it would not go back in without a struggle. 'It's hurting me . . .' she cried, so I took the letter from her and rolled it properly and tried to reinsert it into the bottle. It took a few attempts, as I was distracted by her distress and in my haste failed to roll it tightly enough. At last I managed to slide it through the narrow neck and put the top back on.

'Good,' she sighed in relief. She continued. 'Perhaps the child committed suicide? I see him in the water, I see someone trying to fish out something from the water, someone diving down to the bottom of the water. I think it is a woman. I see a boat, I see a coast, so I think it was thrown in from France, towards Brittany, somewhere like that, perhaps.

'I wonder whether she was in hospital for a while, a psychiatric ward or something . . . I see a woman losing lots of blood, blood from her lower stomach.' She gestured with her hands to show the flow of liquid coming from the woman. 'I can see her being hospitalized. This woman has been in hospital. One can become mad from grief.

'Strange, I can feel something like madness, something rather deranged,' the clairvoyant repeated. 'She is more than perturbed, of course one is perturbed by the death of a child, of course, but this is worse. This is a woman who has gone to the very depths, to a level of consciousness . . .

'I don't feel her any more, I can't feel the woman. Strange because I see her hair, I see her wandering, I see her walking on the coast, I see her drifting all alone. I see someone – a woman who is all alone, maybe divorced or separated, but anyhow all alone. Does she mention in the letter that she is alone?'

'She doesn't mention a man,' I replied.

'In my opinion she is alone. Completely isolated. A woman all alone, very disturbed.' A pause.

'You know, I can see this woman as clearly as I see you. If I were any good at drawing I could draw her. I see a woman with long hair.'

She pointed towards the bottle. 'Hers is the darker of the two locks. Her hair hangs down like this, rather long,' and again she drew her hands straight down the sides of her head.

'Her face is not plump, she is rather thin, her face is a bit hollow.' She sucked in her cheeks. 'Her eyes are fairly pale. I see her drifting a bit, like those slightly mad women one sees, wandering around. I see her walking. I see a little house. A very lonely woman, in a skirt.'

She was in full flow now and needed no prompting. 'She is a lonely woman, who has lived alone, a woman abandoned by men, who has suffered a great deal. Very lonely.

'But she is no fool. She is a simple woman, not very sophisticated, but at the same time, a very intelligent woman, extraordinarily sensitive. A woman in search of love, alone and in despair, in search of love. And also I have the impression that she had only this son to cling to.' Although she had not read the letter, the impression of solitude and of the relationship with the son seemed to be accurate.

229

'The woman wrote the letter because she didn't know with whom to talk. She did it because she was very alone. I see her walking, wandering around on the rocks, on the beaches, all alone, and she needed someone to know her story. This is someone who has confided her despair to the sea. Consigned her grief to the waves.

'I see a coast, like Brittany. I see her wandering, And it is strange, I also see next to her a woman, a mother or a grandmother all in black, like a Breton, a kind of countrywoman . . .

'This is a woman who is very marked by her mother. It is curious, I see in her origins women, many women. There are more women than men in her life.

'Perhaps in her first name there is a J – Janine, Jacqueline, Genevieve. I see a J.

'I see the child . . . I see . . . it's bizarre . . . I have an impression of . . . She doesn't speak at all of what he died?' I shook my head.

'I see a very violent fever, something infectious, something quite devastating, violent. A kind of infection, a virus that carried him off very quickly. I see a fever, I see a child trembling, but I see water at the same time. I can't quite see who is swimming . . .

'I see someone who has a fever, but at the same time someone underwater trying to fish out something, perhaps it is a scene that has nothing to do with the death of the child. I see someone diving. But it's her going under the water, her swimming underwater. I don't think it is someone who drowned, no, not him. He had something like a fever, an infection, something like that. But her, I see her often with her hair, like that, underwater.'

In my own mind's eye I could see the dark-haired, pale-eyed, lonely woman diving from the small boat, swimming down desperately to find something. An active Ophelia, not lying there calmly waiting to drown. The clairvoyant's hands waved beside her head, like seaweed floating in the tide.

'I don't know the story surrounding the water I see. Why is she diving under? Looking for something? I don't know, I can't tell you. But it is not the child I see under the water, because I see her next to the coffin, next to the child. I see him on a bed. The child is on a bed. But why is she diving? Is she looking for something? I don't know. Sometimes I see her on a boat too. I see a great deal of water.

'What's that in the bottle?' she suddenly asked. 'Is it little stones?' I tried to explain about the sweet-smelling sandalwood shavings, but my French vocabulary deserted me and I was left mumbling about 'good-smelling things'.

She nodded. 'I wonder if the thing she is diving for, whether it is not this bottle floating . . . I don't know. There is something very conscious in all this. There is a good deal of planning involved here. The scented bits, the bottle, the two locks of hair. The bottle is lovely. Beautiful. Extraordinarily beautiful. Again I have a terrible headache.

231

I wonder whether the child didn't have something wrong with his head . . . if he had terrible headaches. These headaches, there must be something to do with the head.' I thought about the tarot reader, who had also indicated that the death had been linked in some way to the child's head.

'But it's strange, there is a death. Are you looking for her? Do you want to meet her?'

The sudden question took me by surprise. 'I don't know. I want to know the story,' I stumbled. Did I want to meet her? I no longer knew. I could not foresee any circumstances under which such a meeting would be easy. I think I did not want to meet her, I simply wanted to know the answers, and to know that now she was happier.

'This story has upset you a great deal, hasn't it?'

'Wouldn't anyone be upset who thought about it?' I countered.

'Not necessarily,' she replied, shrugging.

I reflected on that in surprise. I suppose it was true, one could read the letter and remain untouched. I wondered again just why I was spending so much time trying to find her. Was my interest normal? Was I turning into a ghastly stalker? A voyeur? Or perhaps just a bore? A woman with too little to do, too much time to spare?

'Do you write?' she asked suddenly.

'Yes,' I admitted. She could have looked me up on the internet, if she checked her daily appointments, but I doubted it. Earlier she had not seemed to know how to spell my name. After all, I was only one client among many.

'It's not by chance that the bottle came to you. It's as though you are supposed to write about it. That would be a good conclusion for the letter. It's a magnificent story. There is something utterly *romanesque* about it.

'I've had a sudden astonishing thought,' she exclaimed. 'If one day you write a story about this, maybe someone will recognize themselves in it. They might contact you.'

But then she became serious and frowned at her cards again. 'You're going to have problems finding this person. Are you sure she's alive? I see death. For me, this woman is no longer alive.' She paused.

'I don't think you will ever find her,' she said very definitely, staring intently at her cards. 'I don't see her alive any more. For me she is no longer alive.

And abruptly she gathered her cards together, wished me well, and swept from the room. The séance was – very suddenly – over. I packed up the bottle, feeling exhausted, and her secretary silently showed me out.

21

It seemed I had an answer. The letter-writer was, apparently, dead.
And, again according to the self-professed seer, I was to write a
book about her and about my search for her. My quest was, finally, at
an end. I had exhausted the possibilities, explored the live leads and
the dead ends, used both scientific and alternative methods of investigation. I could think of nothing more I could do, short of spending
the rest of my life combing through the records of the 36,000 town
halls of France, and I realized that my obsession had run its course.
Once back in London, I took out the bottle and looked at it, and then
picked up the telephone to call my friend the dog-walker and tell her
it was over.

I had planned to throw the bottle back into the sea to continue
its journey. My friend and I would come to some arrangement with

the Sheerness lifeboat crew. We would travel from the shore where the letter was found to the furthest point of their patrol, where the currents drift northwards to the Arctic. We would be dressed in fleeces and waterproof jackets, but we would probably be cold and damp and miserable. Then, when we had reached the limits of the lifeboat's range, we would take the bottle and hurl it as far as we could, out over the waves. There would be a blue glint of farewell, and then it would be gone, swallowed up in the ocean. In the dull grey, we would look and look, but it would be gone, 'forever rocked by the ocean, in the ebb and flow of the rolling waves . . .'

But what if I had missed something in my researches? What if there were just one more avenue to pursue? What if the writer appeared and wanted the letter back? I realized I was not quite cured. I replaced the bottle in its harbour of tissue paper, cradled in its protective box, and hid it away. I would throw it onwards. But not just yet.

At first I had been sure I would succeed in tracing the letter-writer. My worries had been less about failure and more about how the mother might feel at having her identity revealed. Devastated or pleased? I had also fretted about what she might be like. Would she live up to expectations? Would it not be better to leave her undiscovered? I feared that I might end up meeting not a tragic poet, but someone far more banal and everyday. Although part of me felt that she would be pleased that I had spent so much time looking for her, pleased that we wanted to know about Maurice, pleased that he might live on for other people who had never known him, I did worry that the letter was a form of closure for her and that it would be discourteous to infringe on her grief. And perhaps by writing this book I have.

I have not tried to make a television appeal. I felt I owed it to the unknown mother to make a choice about whether to come forward or to remain anonymous if she hears about my quest through the small ads, or if she comes across my book. Her letter had reached and touched so many of us: my friend the dog-walker, the lady at the statistics office, the Professor's wife, the graphologist, most of the people to whom I had spoken, and perhaps those of you who have followed my quest. Above all, she had touched me, and I look at my own children and give thanks for them, and I worry about them and their fragile mortality, and I worry about the unknown letter-writer, hidden in the shadows, sharing her grief only with her friend Christine and the shade of Maurice. A grief that in her loneliness she consigned to the 'dark illimitable ocean without bound' to float on for evermore . . . But that ocean, 'Without dimension, where length, breadth, and highth and time and place are lost', betrayed her and almost immediately spat the bottle up on an English beach.

Perhaps the clairvoyant was right and the Frenchwoman was dead.

It was strange that in spite of my researches I had found no real echo of her continued existence. Did I really believe in the clairvoyant's predictions? I no longer knew what I thought.

But if, somewhere, the letter-writer is alive, then perhaps this book can serve as a clumsy 'letter-in-a-bottle' reply.

To Maurice's mother, wherever you are. The sea brought your bottle to me. I read your letter. It moved me. It made me weep for you and with you. I hope that your grief will grow more bearable with time. I hope with all my heart that you have found happiness.

I wonder if she will receive my message.

'I too but signify at the utmost a little wash'd-up drift,

A few sands and dead leaves to gather,

Gather, and merge myself as part of the sands and drift.'

Walt Whitman, 'As I Ebb'd with the Ocean of Life', 1860

Original Transcript: The Letter

A tous les navires au large, à tous les ports d'attache, à ma famille, à tous les amis et à tous les inconnus.

Ceci est un message, une prière, le message, c'est que mes souffrances, mes enonces m'ont enseignées une grande verité.

J'avais déjà ce que tout le monde recherche (il y a bien longtemps) ... et que peu arrivent de trouver, la seule personne au monde que je suis née pour aimer toute ma vie, mon premier fils, Maurice, un enfant riche de trésors tout simple, et que nul vent ... , nulle tempête ... , ni même la mort ne pourront jamais détruire, la prière ... c'est que toutes les mères puissant connaitre un tel amour afin qu'ils les guèrissent ... Si ma prière est exaucée, elle effacera, toutes fautes ... tous regrets ... et apaisera toutes colères.

S'il vous plait mon dieu ...

Ma vie a commencé avec lui à sa naissance, et j'ai cru qu'elle était finie quand il m'a quitté un soir d'été pour ne plus jamais revenir, il avait treize ans ... sans prevenir, il s'est dérobé à la vie dans un trop plein de désirs, un trop vif de vivance, à l'aurore de l'été. Il a voyagé longtemps entre deux eaux, entre deux lumières, pour tenter d'eteindre infatigablement le repos de ses deux bras tendus. Il a subi, le silence, les peurs et le froid, mais il a découvert les chemins secrets de l'univers, le mouvement infini des origines, et l'enonce des étoiles.

Il ne savait pas que moi, sa mere je l'alimentais de mes pensées pour lui donner inlassablement la vie en souvenir, pour le garder en entire au present de ma chair.

Pardon mon fils, mon amour ... , j'ai cru qu'en accrochant ainsi à ton souvenir, je nous maintiendrais en vie tous les deux aussi longtemps que possible. Pardon mon fils de ne pas t'avoir parlé depuis si longtemps, j'avais le sentiment d'être perdue, sans repère, je n'arrêtais pas de me cogner, de trébucher partout ... , jamais avant que tu ne me quittes, je m'avais été perdue, c'était toi qui m'indiquais le nord, je retrouvais toujours mon chemin, car tu étais mon chemin.

Pardonne la colère qu'a été ta disparition, je pense toujours qu'une erreur a été commise et j'attends de Dieu qu'il la répare.

Je vais mieux maintenant mon grand, le chemin a été long, très long, mais par dessous tout, c'est toi que me soutiens.

Tu m'es apparu en rêve, il y a quelque nuits, et tu avais le sourire qui me berce comme une enfant, j'ai compris qu'il était temps pour moi de te laisser partir.

Tu es resté près de moi pendant toutes ces années ... , je me suis accrochée avec toute ma désespèrance à ce qui n'était plus et qui me sera jamais plus.

Mon infinitude, j'ai commence par laisser s'échapper de mon être, de mon Coeur, de mon âme, cette souffrance qui m'habitait entièrement croyant qu'elle me reliait à toi, ne laissant place à rien d'autre. J'ai réussi grace à toi mon amour, à transformer cette souffrance en amour, en vivance. Tout ce que j'ai gardé du rêve, c'est un sentiment de paix, pour oit, mour moi, à mon réveil, je l'éprouvais encore et je me suis efforcée de le prolonger aussi longtemps que possible.

Je t'écris Maurice, pour te dire que je m'embarque à la recherche de cette paix, et pour te demander pardon pour tant de choses. Pardon de n'avoir pas su te protéger de la mort, pardon de n'avoir pas su trouver les mots dans ce terrible moment où tu me glissais entre les doigts, pour exprimer ce que je ressentais et par dessous tout de n'avoir pas su te serrer si fort que dieu n'aurait pu t'emporter.

Il n'est pas un instant de ma vie mon fils où tu ne sois present. Que de chemins traversés avant de pouvoir écouter et entendre le son de ma souffrance, de notre souffrance.

Tes treizes années de vie m'ont apporté un bonheur infini.

Aujourd'hui, je sais que tu as été de passage pour me montrer un chemin, pour témoigner d'un choix de vie à faire, tu m'as invite par ton depart, d'oser un changement que je n'avais pas envisagé jusqu'alors. Tu avais le pouvoir de dire, par ta présence vie, combine furtive et fugace et ta disparition brutale, maman 'oses ta vie, toi seule la vivras'. J'écoute et j'entends auhourd'hui le message que mon fils m'a envoyé, dont la présence si ephemère m'a blessée à jamais en restant sourde longtemps à son message.

Aujourd'hui le voyage se termine, mon fils a regagné le port, près d'un rivage lointain, tout près du soleil levant. Il a retrouvé la barque légère de son enfance qui le conduira doucement vers la paix conquise.

Voilà mon grand, mon amour, je laisse s'envoler le ballon vers les cieux, sereinement avec toute ma tendresse de maman.

Que cette bouteille, jetée au large des côtes, reste à jamais bercée par les flots, dans le va et vient des vagues déferlantes.

Tant que Dieu me prêtera vie, je te promets de vivre et d'exister pleinement, de savourer chaque instant de ma vie dans la plenitude et la sérénité.

Je sais que nous nous retrouverons, quand le moment sera venu, Dieu nous doit bien cela.

Au revoir mon fils, au revoir mon amour.

Je t'aime de tout mon Coeur, de toute mon âme et je suis fière d'avoir été ta maman. Tu peux t'envoler dans la quietude.

Vas mon amour, vas vers la lumière, mon doux goêland. Que la source de ton âme jaillisse et court en murmurant vers la mer, et se déplie comme un lotus aux petales inombrables.

L'histoire de la plupart d'entre-nous, s'écrit probablement à l'improviste, au fur et à mesure que nous parcourons le chemin de la vie, mais il ait des existences qui semblent tracées d'avance, ineluctable et qui forment un cercle parfait. Il en ait d'autres dont le trace est imprévisible, parfois incomprehensible. Ce que j'ai eu le chagrin de perdre au cours de ma vie m'a enseigné ce qu'il y a de plus précieux comme me l'a enseigné un amour qui m'emplit de gratitude.

Cette lettre mon fils, je tiens à le partager avec une seule personne, la seule amie que je garderais toute ma vie et bien au delà, elle s'appelle Christine, elle est la douceur infinie.

This is a transcript of the original letter and grammatical oddities have not been amended.

The Letter in the Bottle

The Search Concludes

Three Years Later

The first edition of *The Letter in the Bottle* was published in English in 2006. There were a couple of good reviews and a small flurry of emails, mainly from South Africa, all asking whether I had anything new to add since publication. But none provided any further information.

The years passed and the mystery remained. I did not forget my quest, and I retained a 'Google alert' on key phrases –'lettre dans une bouteille', 'bouteille à la mer', 'Maurice, 13 ans'. Daily updates about the Île Maurice, Maurice Pialat, Maurice Jarre and so forth dropped into my inbox. But I made no other efforts and I moved on with my life.

The French edition was published in May 2009. By then my children were in their mid and late-teens and I was in the midst of something else. I re-read my book, now in a mellifluous translation that made it sound – at least to my Anglo-Saxon ears – far more lyrical and poignant. Or perhaps it was just that I was further removed from events now, three years later. The publisher assured me that there would be press coverage but the weeks passed and no one was interested. Suddenly I got a call: a national French newspaper wanted to interview me and my friend Sioux where she had found the bottle, on the beach on the Isle of Sheppey.

I hadn't talked to Sioux for a couple of years. There had been a misunderstanding, nothing to do with the letter in the bottle, more to do with our differences in personality and aspirations. Now I sent her a tentative email, expecting her to delete it immediately, but she replied as though nothing had ever happened to our relationship. Yes, she would meet us on the beach; all was fine.

I met the journalist and photographer off the shuttle in Ashford. We rented a car that I was to drive, as they feared the English wrong-hand drive. I had borrowed a sat-nav that failed to function and that kept interjecting with inappropriate directions. The screen remained stuck on the first image, and we had brought no paper map. The photographer snored on the back seat, exhausted it seemed by his previous night's carousing. I drove around Kent under increasing stress, trying to find the Isle of Sheppey, while the journalist interviewed me in speedy colloquial French and the sat-nav firmly ordered me to turn at non-existent junctions. It was not a relaxing drive.

When we arrived at the beach the wind was blowing with a gale force. The tide was in and there was no beach. The waves were high, the air full of spray. Sioux was already there with a new dog, her old companions having passed away in the intervening years. The photographer asked me to take out the letter from the bottle and pose near the water. I could hardly hear his instructions over the wind. The journalist ran back to take refuge in the car, while my friend and I tried to follow the photographer's curt orders. Between the spray and the wind the letter began to suffer. The wind was so strong I couldn't even open my eyes, and my nose and eyes began to run with horizontal moisture. The dog decided she had had enough and ran away. In the pictures, published in the paper two days later, my hair is vertical in the wind. In the background Sioux and her dog look in opposite directions, my friend out to sea, her long blonde hair whipping madly around her head, the dog gazing longingly back inland, visibly shivering.

As soon as the article appeared, media interest exploded. Two national TV channels sent crews to film us, once more back on the same beach, but this time in calmer weather conditions, with the tide out and a grey beach visible. We repeated the same story each time.

The breakthrough came after the very first TV interview was screened. Olivier, the psychologist who ran the website www.bouteilleàlamer.com rang. He had never telephoned before. We had remained friendly, and he had left the search notice posted on his website throughout the intervening years. No one had ever got in touch with him. 'I've been contacted by someone. I think it's genuine.'

My heart stopped; how true a cliché can be. I struggled to take a breath, an active encouragement from brain to lungs to breathe once more.

'She sent an email to my site,' he explained. 'She said "I am the person who threw this bottle in 2002" followed by a telephone number. I was stupefied!'

I sat down, shocked, amazed, thrilled. In the background, he continued to talk: 'I read the message at least five times to be sure that I was not dreaming, then the questions flooded in: "Was it the real person? Why contact me when your email address is in the back of the book so people can contact you directly? What should I do?"'

He told me he would not pass on her number, but would immediately ring her himself.

'Yes,' I whispered. 'Good luck. Let me know.' And then I sat by the telephone, unable to focus on anything, waiting until he rang me back. An hour later, the phone rang once more.

'I'm sure it's her. As soon as she picked up the phone, I was gripped by the tone of her voice, the authenticity of her manner of speaking.'

Olivier told me that her son – her son? she had another son? – had seen me on the news, recognized his mother's writing on the letter and told her to go immediately and check out the news replayed on the Internet. She had then rushed out to buy the book and read it in state of shock. She told him she found him one of the few sympathetic voices in the book, and had decided to contact him as an intermediary.

'I had no further doubt that she was the author,' he explained. 'The voice, the words were those of a woman who was simultaneously fragile and strong. She said that she had just learnt that a woman had been seeking her for seven years, that a book had been written about her letter in the bottle. Henceforth the whole world knew her letter, and it was as though her story, her suffering, her very intimate being no longer belonged to her. She says she felt as though she has been violated.'

I was devastated. 'It was not meant like that. Please, can I talk to her?'

'I did ask her whether she would talk to you, meet you. Maybe . . . definitely . . . but not yet, she needs time. She needs space, maybe a few months, an intermediary perhaps. That was why she contacted me.'

I sent a message back to her via Olivier that of course I would respect her wishes. I was terribly upset that her reaction was one of 'violation', but felt that if I could gain enough trust to talk to her directly we could rectify the situation, make it all better.

Meanwhile I realized that I had to carry on with my interviews and publicity as though nothing had happened. If I refused, it would be obvious that something dramatic had occurred, and I would have to explain that she, the author of the letter, the unknown mother, had emerged. And she was not ready. Neither was I. So I told no one except my family. It was surreal and rather horrible.

Two days later I was on live lunchtime news. 'Do you think you'll ever find her?' '[Yes, I already have.] I hope so.' 'What will she think of you?' '[She'll be appalled.] I hope she'll understand.' 'Will she be surprised you've spent so long hunting for her?' '[She'll think I'm a mad stalker, barely one level up from a rapist.] I suppose so, after all, it has been seven years.'

My responses were addressed to both the interviewer and the audience at home, and also of course to the unknown mother. A stereo of double and triple entendres that exhausted me, added to which everything was in a foreign language. However, in some way this helped, since at least the French media personalities who interviewed me were unknown to me, and I was completely unimpressed by their celebrity. It all felt like a dream, a parallel universe where I was recognized in the street and my mobile phone never stopped ringing. As soon as I returned to England I stepped back once more into my true identity as a nobody.

The unknown mother had asked for time to come to terms with the news. Perhaps in the future she would talk to me, but for now I continued on my media treadmill. *France Culture*, a radio station equivalent to Radio 4 in the UK wanted to interview me. The producer and I, accompanied by her intern, a young girl on work experience, walked to Parc Monceau. We meandered through the artificial landscape of lawns and ruined follies looking for somewhere to sit amidst the countless Philippino nannies chattering away on their mobile phones, as their pale white charges played around them, taking care not to dirty their beautiful clothes. We found a bench overlooking a glade where some older ladies were practising t'ai chi, and began to talk. We sat there for two and a half hours, during which I used every word of my rusty French 'A' level vocabulary. The t'ai chi ladies left, and a handsome young Rasta with loose trousers and a cut-off T-shirt took their place on the lawn before us and began to practise his karate moves, handstands and balances, his T-shirt falling upwards to reveal a finely muscled torso. I continued to mumble about parental bereavement to the insistent microphone held under my nose, but suddenly it was all too much for the intern. Silently and abruptly she left our bench and introduced herself to the Rasta with a few rudimentary cartwheels. Soon – sooner than one could have believed possible – she was lying on her back on the grass, the Rasta's head on her bare stomach, stroking his matted hair with a loving hand. The producer and I sat astonished on the bench and tried to focus on the interview, muffling our giggles.

Somehow the little scene represented the force of life; the sparrows – almost extinct in my home town of London – were chirping around us, the pigeons were courting their mates, and the strength of spring-time sexual attraction was just too strong to withstand. I thought of earlier days in other parks, when I too had practised my karate, and smiled. Later the intern would be made to ring me and apologise, and her voice would read the letter – beautifully – on the half-hour radio programme, as though she were a bereaved mother, rather than a happy-go-lucky student with only one thing on her mind. And all the time I was being interviewed I had to hide the fact that someone had made contact with me, and would almost certainly turn out to be the unknown mother.

A month passed. I received a great deal of mail, most of it electronic, the occasional beautifully calligraphed letter, some even written in purple ink. They fell into different categories. There were those wished to help. A night shift lorry driver sent me detailed graphs about the distribution and popularity of the name Maurice, *départe-ment* by *département*, decade by decade. A reader 'with the soul of a detective' concluded that the mother would have been between thirty and fifty-five years old in 2001. Therefore she would be born between 1946 and 1971; meaning her son would have been born between 1983 and 1988. Using data from INSEE, the National Institute of Statistics and Economic Studies, he concluded that thirty-seven Maurices were born along the northern coasts of France between these dates, and I had only to ask each maternity hospital for their help. 'Within a few days you will have found her,' he summarised blithely, surely underestimating the constraints of patient confidentiality.

A couple of readers suggested new and unrealistically time-consuming lines of research that I had failed to explore. The film *Message in a Bottle* had been sent out a few years earlier as a free sample by a mail order company – perhaps the company could tell me to whom they had sent it? Perhaps Metro could supply a list of their trade suppliers and I could track the bottle through them? Perhaps I could try school registers? Others sent me their theories about how the child had died and why the mother had done what she had done.

A couple of readers had specific tips: a neighbour of their mother's called Jeannette (the letter that the medium had identified as being the first initial) had lost a child called Maurice during the last years of the war. Later the mother had emigrated to Cap Vert and the correspondent suggested that she had perhaps written the letter in the bottle when leaving the land where her first son was buried. The correspondent planned to wade through all her past letters in case she had received a letter or a card from Jeannette so that we could compare the handwriting. Another thought he had heard something about a similar bottle while working on a patrol boat for the Lighthouse and Radio Beacon Service in Brittany.

One girl sent me a scan of a sad letter dated February 1946 that she had found under a floor board in her parents' attic, saying she had been inspired by my search to seek out the author and return the letter to him, though it seemed likely that too many years had passed. An eighty-five-year old gentleman sent me a beautiful graph of the letters he had sent in bottles. Between 1984 and 2004 he had sent nearly 1500 bottles, receiving 258 replies, an 18% success rate. The graph tabulated the country of origin of the reply – top place to Algeria with forty-nine, closely followed by France and Tunisia – and the time of receipt, with 1992 being a vintage year of twenty-four replies.

Only one reader strongly disapproved. A Swiss man emailed to say how shocked he had been at my search, and asked me how I had dared to hunt the mother like prey when she had clearly sought anonymity and closure. Perhaps he was right.

Many told me of their emotions on reading the book; how moved they had been by the letter, or of how it had helped them in some way. Some wrote how they too had lost a child, or simply how they had come to appreciate their children more after reading of the heart-breaking loss of the young boy.

But mostly there were those who simply wanted to know if there had been any progress, to request an update, to put down a marker that I should let them know if the story were to reach a definite conclusion at some point in the future. As I read the letters, and sent back short responses, I was just waiting for the call from the unknown mother. Could she forgive me enough to get in contact directly, to let me speak to her and try to explain?

Then, almost one month to the day after the first contact, the psychologist rang me again. 'She is ready. You can ring her.'

I needed a day to steady my nerves, then rang the number he had given me. As soon as I said 'Bonjour,' she replied: 'Bonjour Karen.' A strange conversation, between two people who were now inextricably linked, and who in a way knew a great deal about the other person – me from her letter, she from my media appearances – but who were nevertheless completely unknown to one another. After some awkward introductory formalities, we spent the rest of the conversation arranging where we would meet the following week. I passed the intervening time in a state of high anxiety. I know she did too.

I arrived several hours early for the ferry to France and would have had time to climb the white cliffs of Dover three times, had my overnight bag not been so heavy. The crossing was uneventful and I arrived at my little hotel without incident. I went for a walk around the town centre to calm my nerves and then retired to my dingy room to watch rubbishy French television, trying not to notice – or touch – the ominous stains on the blanket and carpets that recalled previous meals or worse, previous sexual encounters. When I pulled back the sheets on the bed, something with too many legs half-scuttled, half-hopped away under the pillow. I did not sleep well.

The next morning I took my breakfast and sat myself in the bar as instructed. I had a view across the road, and as the hour of our appointment drew near I began nervously to watch the women approaching. Would she come alone, or with her companion? Was this lumpy peasant woman carrying bags of shopping my date? Or this stolid stony-faced older couple marching glumly down the road, looking neither to left nor right?

In fact she approached from a different angle, and I didn't see her until she was inside the bar, her companion behind her. She hesitated a moment, framed in the doorway, and we looked at one another in silence before she came forward. She was very pretty, slim and elegant, with a delicate face and good cheekbones, of medium height and wearing white linen trousers with a loose flowing top. Her hair was dark brown and she wore it in a loose bob. I didn't try to guess her age at that point and though she later told me she was sixty, she looked much younger. As she stood at the door her whole body and bearing seemed to radiate tension and worry. We immediately recognized one another, but it was not difficult: she had seen me on the television and I was waiting for someone to approach me in a quiet bar in a provincial French town at ten in the morning. I drew a shaky breath as she approached my table, both of us smiling nervously. Behind her, her *compagnon* hovered protectively, a compact man with closely cropped grey hair and a no-nonsense handshake.

We sat down together and looked at one another, both silent, overcome and dumbstruck by the occasion. After searching for so many years, I could not believe I was there, face to face with the author of the letter.

And so we talked. We spent the whole day together. All morning we talked, and Olivier, our intermediary, joined us for lunch. The mystery was solved. And though she would answer all my questions with a breath-taking, heart-breaking honesty and permit me to share them in this book, she begged that I keep her identity secret. She hadn't written the letter for any kind of acknowledgement or discovery; on the contrary. But now that it had happened, the story could still become "une belle histoire", a happy ending, but she insisted that her identity remain secret. I promised, and I dearly hope it does.

Conclusion

Meeting the unknown mother was an extraordinary and moving experience. She had become the mythical treasure pot at the end of the rainbow, a goal that one can never reach. She was just a fictional character in a book I had once written. It was a shock to meet a real live human being, a person who had suffered terribly, and perhaps was continuing to do so because of my insensitive search for her.

I was surprised that she was so amazed that someone had found her letter in a bottle. It was a letter: after all – a letter is usually written to be sent, written to be delivered, written to be read. She had seen the film *Message in a Bottle*, where the journalist finds the letters and publishes them in her newspaper, leading to huge press interest . . . Why had she been so surprised? Although I felt guilty and worried that I was re-opening healed wounds for her, I also felt that – especially given the context of the film that had clearly meant so much for her that she had included lines drawn from it in her letter – she should have expected that someone might find and read the letter.

The first error I had made had been the date when Sioux found the bottle. She had found it on the beach, kept it for a few weeks, then sent it to me; I had kept it for a few weeks before translating it. Later, when I realised I was on a serious trail looking for the author, we had tried to remember the date that Sioux found it – and we had made a mistake, thinking the bottle had been found in February. In fact, the mother had only thrown it into the sea in March – she showed me the ferry tickets that she had carefully kept – and we had found the bottle barely a few days later. This was my first, and most glaring error. The lifeguard had been right in his favoured assumption – that it had been thrown from a cross-Channel ferry. That meant that all those who had 'seen' the mother on the cliffs, hurling the bottle, such as the tarot reader, were wrong.

My search for statistical information on the deaths of thirteen year-olds had been misguided too, as I had partially realized after a few weeks, because Maurice had not drowned. At the time they had been living in central France, although she had later moved to a town along the northern French shore. The watery imagery had been used only because the mother had always loved the sea, and because of its poetic associations.

All my days spent hunting through the death notices of the local newspapers had been in vain. The experts had suggested at least five years mourning for a child, but in fact it had taken her a massive twenty-one years to write the letter. The 'dawn of summer' was just a lyrical expression, perhaps (as one reader suggested to me) indicating that he was leaving childhood and entering adulthood, and my searches through the months of May and June (quite apart from being sixteen years too late) were also wasted, since Maurice had died in August.

The name 'Maurice' itself contained no clues. 'I didn't choose the name Maurice', she told me. 'At the maternity hospital I called him Emmanuel, and my husband went to register him; the maternity nurse came bursting in a few days later saying, "How can you do this to your little wife, who has been in labour for three days." He had named him Maurice, after his own father. In my heart he remained Emmanuel.'

Together the mother and I began to look through the evidence of the so-called experts whose advice I had sought. In each chapter there were some small elements of truth, but in general what we both found striking was how much they got wrong. In fact we were shocked at the erroneous analysis offered, the kind of advice that they must also be offering – usually for money – to vulnerable clients seeking their advice. As we sat there going through the book, I thought how surreal and intrusive it must feel to read such a strange and unsolicited in-depth analysis about your own character and life, let alone such a misguided one!

The psychoanalytic psychotherapist had wondered whether the mother and child had perhaps been too close, and it seems she had been right about the bond between mother and son. The husband was not mentioned in the letter, not because he did not exist but because, she explained, the letter was not addressed to him. It was addressed to Maurice, or at least to the rest of the world, the sea, the universe. 'All this stuff about the son becoming a substitute for all her emotional and erotic needs – theoretically he becomes the phallus . . . this is all rubbish,' said the mother in a tone of outrage. All the talk of rupture, alienation, breaking attachments, conflicts – this was all false. 'I was never in conflict with my son at all. We listened to music together, we did painting together. The therapist must have transposed her own conflicts onto my relationship with my son. And she thinks there are no other men in my life, but with a husband and three other sons, she is very wrong. The only part she was right about was that I had been in therapy'. Turning to her companion with a gentle smile she said, 'Look, she thinks I have turned away from men . . . Not at all,' she said, smiling at him. 'Not at all.'

263

The boy had been killed cycling in a simple and horrible twist of fate. A disastrously extended domestic chore which meant that the parents were out for longer than expected buying a new TV had led indirectly to a terrible road accident. No one was to blame, no one had in any Lacanian way facilitated events. It was just one of those terrible things that fate flings out.

The 'momentous' mention of Christine, with its suggested lesbian overtones also proved to be only the result of an over-active imagination, both from the psychotherapist and from my friend. She and Christine had had a good laugh over it – probably one of the few laughs they got from the book. Married with two children, Christine was, in the words of the mother, 'my best friend, my soul mate, closer than my sister.' Later I would meet Christine and see their friendship for myself. Together they had been through a lot, and they had travelled some kind of spiritual voyage together. But there was no physical element to their relationship.

The Professor of Literature had seen the mother as relatively uneducated in a formal sense, and this had turned out to be true. Though the psychotherapist had imagined her to be a 'Catholic woman from a high-class French family' and the graphologist had analysed her as being highly educated, in fact the unknown woman, daughter of a welder, had left school at fourteen and become a mother while still in her teens. She had been a shop assistant and a receptionist.

According to her, the Professor of French Literature was one of the few experts to analyse her letter with any degree of accuracy or insight, a view possibly coloured by his appreciation for her use of language and his praise for the poetry of some of her phrasing. He had correctly identified nineteenth-century poetry as a source of inspiration for her, and she agreed with his analysis. 'Victor Hugo in particular was a great influence. I have always been fascinated by him. He lost a daughter, Léopoldine, who drowned in the Seine, and his style was imprinted on mine.'

The little ticks along the top of the letter represented seagulls. 'I've always loved seagulls, to me they symbolise freedom. And the sign of infinity, means something special to me. It's a link with my family background.' But apart from that she reserved particular scorn for the graphologist's analysis. "A lack of imagination [absolutely not, on the contrary it is overflowing], a relatively high level of education [absolutely not, I'm an auto-didact], not disorientated by sickness or medication [at that time I was taking medication, so she's wrong there], a feeling for numbers . . . probably an accountant [on the contrary, I absolutely hate numbers], this is not someone who would grab her rucksack [on the contrary, I just did a pilgrimage to Compostela]." I queried the pilgrimage and she explained that she had walked 850km, 25km a day for thirty-three days, to say farewell to her father. 'My father came from the Pays Basque, so I wanted to walk to the land of my father. For my son I achieved closure by sending the bottle; for my father I did this long walk. There was nothing Catholic about it, I just love walking. So the graphologist was wrong there. And she says I have a masculine side – I absolutely don't agree with that, I think I'm very feminine.' And indeed, looking at her, with her pretty face and mannerisms, her attractive clothing and shoes, and her adoring companion, I had to agree.

We looked at one another, and suddenly the surreal aspect hit us both – there we were, two women who had barely met, two quite private women, sitting together discussing the most intimate elements of one of their lives, based on a private tragedy and a private action, as analysed by a faraway graphologist. So were the graphologist's findings 'the ramblings of a well-meaning amateur' as I had postulated, or a convincing description of the unknown woman? I have to say it seems to me that they were both. There was a lot of rubbish in the analysis, but there was some that both the mother and I conceded was true. For instance, 'The sense of a thick, almost suffocating layer of control, plastered over an emotional cauldron' seemed spot on. But overall the hit rate of accuracy for the graphologist was barely an unimpressive 50 per cent.

We continued to look through the analyses in the book. I had investigated the possibility of DNA testing. 'I was so shocked by that,' said the mother. The DNA results could only have provided an identity to the boy if he had had a criminal record. 'Maurice never had any problems with the police. That really shocked me, that made me feel quite ill. He was a healthy boy, there were never any problems like that.'

The tarot reader also received short shrift: 'She says that in the second stage of my life I was blocked, not knowing how to go on. Well, I was thirty-two when Maurice died, I'm sixty now, so perhaps that refers to the accident? Then came a change and a third stage – what does that mean? She has enormous reserves of energy and vitality – that's all false. She also thinks I'm androgynous – no, I disagree.'

'You're certainly not to me,' interjected her *compagnon*, and she smiled gratefully at him.

'"I do a job involving physical movement" – no. Dynamic, energetic – no. I've "known paradise" – false. This is all complete rubbish. All this stuff about the bottle "overflowing with gaiety, bubbling with happiness" – rubbish. "Problems springing from his father, or his lack of a father" – all false. The father was present, he was quite strict with them, but he was certainly present. "Maurice and his mother had lived together almost as a couple" – that's a shocking thing to say. "He felt protective towards me" – all my children feel protective towards me. "All fire and flames, ready to try anything" – absolutely not. "He was born under Aries" – no, he was not, he was born on 18th June.'

She turned to me with an expression of disdain on her face. 'The graphologist and the tarot reader; there's really not much worth hearing from either of them.'

Then we turned our attention to the medium. 'She seemed very exuberant, very dramatic, very theatrical,' said the *compagnon*. The medium had described someone with longish hair, slim, which was accurate. The pale eyes were wrong. So were many other things: '"Swimming underwater" – I hate swimming, I never put my face in the water. "Death linked to violence of a man" – no. "Bottle thrown from a sailing boat . . . violence on the boat . . . the child committed suicide, a woman losing lots of blood from her stomach . . . a woman drifting all alone . . . a woman abandoned by men . . . a Breton mother or grandmother . . . a name beginning with 'J', 'G' – all this is completely false. "I don't think you will ever find her . . . she is no longer alive." Well, I am alive and you have found me, so all this is false.'

I had a stronger word for the medium's analysis. In fact all the 'alternative' analyses – from the Lacanian therapist to the tarot reader, the graphologist, the astrologer and the medium seemed to me to fall into the same bag. I had always felt their interpretations were dubious but I had given them the benefit of the doubt and now it seemed to me that they had been conclusively proven to be rubbish. It wasn't that they themselves didn't believe in their chosen methods. They saw images in their minds, just like I see images in my mind. The difference is that I know my image is an image, something drawn from my imagination, that may or may not have a bearing on reality, depending on fluke and evidential circumstances. But they see an image and they believe it is reality. They charge their clients – the only people I had paid had been the graphologist, the tarot-reader and astrologer, and the medium – the others had helped out of intellectual curiosity or friendship. But other clients would surely be more vulnerable and open to persuasion than I was. How many of my friends had assured me that I must visit these people, that I would certainly find the answer to my quest? Instead these 'experts' had come up with something closely resembling drivel. As we reached that conclusion, perfectly on cue, the phone rang and it was Olivier saying he had arrived for lunch.

Olivier had been very touched to be invited to join us. Later he wrote to me: 'As soon as I saw her that day I recognized her. She was just what I had imagined from the sound of her voice. Seeing you both together, I truly had the feeling that I was a privileged witness to a meeting that only the tides of the ocean could have brought about. When we all set off for a restaurant to have lunch. I walked between you and HER, feeling like an atom of oxygen between two hydrogen atoms. After a long voyage of seven years, the ink in the bottle was somehow transformed into a water molecule. And in spite of the sun, which shone brightly that day, our drop of water did not evaporate. All the suffering contained in that letter in the bottle, all the pain of losing a child, all the force of despair, transformed itself on that day into a magnificent moment of life.

'Throwing a bottle into the sea is simultaneously wanting to be heard without wanting to be read, or maybe revealed naked. It is an act of relief, sometimes the ultimate relief when faced with the unbearable. I hope that this meeting of you two women will push this letter in the bottle a little further, may it be just the beginning of a long voyage, a beautiful and uncommon story.

'Only those who receive a letter in a bottle can decide whether to be the final recipient. By writing your book you made of each reader a final recipient, a possible somebody somewhere, for the person who one day threw a bottle into the sea.

'And through this voyage, in spite of, and beyond death, a child continues on his path. And thanks to this letter in a bottle, "rocked by the ocean", rocked by the written word, it offers to each mother the most beautiful of messages: that of hope, that of life.'

The four of us – the mother and her *compagnon*, the psychologist and I – went for lunch in the town square. It was one of the earliest days of summer and we happily sat outside where it was pleasant and fresh. As we ate and chatted and my French began to fade in weariness, the town square began to fill up with hundreds of schoolchildren. It was a celebration of the approaching end of the school year, and all the schools in town spilled their children, dressed in matching T-shirts depending on their school and year group, into the town square. The sun came out and began to bake the psychologist and me, while the other two – the mother and her *compagnon* – sat just under the shade of the awning.

By the end of lunch Olivier's face and forehead, and my neck and shoulders were an angry red, and in the following weeks the skin would peel off to remind us of a surreal but lovely lunch. As he later wrote: 'I will never forget the moments of conversation, of reflection with HER, which proved to be one of the precious and lasting gifts that the day offered. And I thank the sun for having engraved this day on my forehead, like a red-hot iron. Yesterday, we had never seen one another, but today and for a long time to come the sun's seal of recognition was branded onto us.'

Conversation, as far as I could follow it through the din of the children, was wide-ranging, easy and interesting. The mother and I were quiet, emotionally drained by our meeting, but the men were ready to talk and the food was good. I found my attention floating away, and I found myself looking surreptitiously at her.

How amazing that I had found her. How amazing that she had agreed to meet, that she had managed to overcome her outrage at what I had done, what I had written. That we had been able to chuckle together and share our irritation at the erroneous analyses and conclusions in the book. How shocking and bizarre must it have been to have one's private tragedy exposed in such a way, and what generosity of spirit had she shown in meeting with me. How beautiful that we could sit in the sun and break bread together, and chat and laugh, and find that we had much in common, although much of it was perforce linked to the death of her son. That perhaps out of that death would come something lasting. 'I want this to be a good story – "une belle histoire",' was the first message that she had sent to me via Olivier.

Out of this tragic and convoluted tale of love, mourning, obsession and stubbornness, had come something beautiful; a memory of a young boy, innocent and gentle. She showed me the last photo, of a boy in a red T-shirt with a wide smile and bright eyes, dark hair lightened by the August sun at the end of the summer holidays. A boy who had had a happy, fulfilled and much-loved childhood, and who had tragically been killed on the last days of his holiday, the last days of his childhood. And a mother who had been almost destroyed by the disaster, but who had rebuilt herself through enormous effort and suffering, though it had taken her more than two decades to do so, and had come through as a person of generosity, humour and beauty of soul.

I can hardly bear to tell you, and I suppose that many of you will not believe me, but on the ferry back to England, after that very first meeting, I saw a pod of dolphins leaping out of a mirror-calm sea. I've crossed the channel many times, and I've never seen anything but seagulls and debris. I couldn't believe my eyes, but the whole ferry-load of passengers saw it too and gasped in amazement, and it was a beautiful thing. Of course I don't believe in such things, but it really did seem like a good sign.

This book is dedicated to Maurice.

The Mother's Story

We took the 11.15 ferry from Calais to Dover on 29 March 2002. The ship was called *Le Renoir* and we stayed on it at Dover. Christine is my best friend, she helped me, she accompanied me. Without her I wouldn't have had the strength to do it. On the way over I tried, but I just didn't have the strength, I simply couldn't bring myself to do it. Then on the way back Christine said, 'You must do it now, throw the bottle now.' So we went up to the bridge, but there were too many people, it was impossible, I just couldn't do it in a crowd.

Suddenly, a few moments later, the bridge emptied of people and we were left alone. It was almost magical. The moment I had prepared for had finally arrived. The first thing I threw over was a bundle of his clothing, the clothes in which he had been killed, his accident clothes. It was so hard; I was screaming, howling, as I did it. I felt I was ripping out my heart, tearing out an essential part of myself. Then came three white lilies that I had brought. I threw them in next.

Finally I threw the bottle into the sea. It disappeared in the wake very quickly, and a sort of pinkish colour spread around the waves where I had thrown it in. Just as the colour began to fade, a group of young people came up on to the bridge, about fifteen of them, and began to sing. Christine said, 'They are singing for your son.' They hadn't seen us throw the bottle, they were singing something beautiful, in English. It was as though choreographed. A magical, sublime moment.

We went back in, shaken, cold and exhausted, and got a coffee. Suddenly in front of us stood another group of young people, wearing T-shirts with numbers on their backs. It had been twenty-one years since Maurice died, it had taken me twenty-one years to come to terms with my suffering, to get to the point where I was ready to let him go. There in front of me stood a boy with a T-shirt with '21' written on his back, right before my eyes, as we sat there with our coffee. Then he was joined, on either side by two other boys, T-shirt '1' on one side, and T-shirt '3' on the other. Together they read '13'; the age at which Maurice had died. Thirteen, encircling twenty-one. It was a strange, magical, moment. They stood in front of me all unknowing, as Christine and I sat there, recovering from the experience on the bridge.

I went home and tried to pick up my normal life once more. But only two days after my return, I was taking my morning shower and I noticed something stinging me, burning me, here on my chest, just below my heart. And when I looked down, there was a burn in the shape of the steering helm of a boat, a circle with thirteen rays. I showed it to the nurse, and she was astonished, she said it was inexplicable, but that I should just accept it, that something had been burnt into me, body and soul. It lasted for about two months, forming a scab, like any other burn, before it finally healed and faded away.

For two or three months after that I was completely empty, destabilised. Maurice died in 1981 and it had taken me twenty-one years to give birth to this suffering; now I had nothing left. After a few months, however, I began to feel liberated. Although one is, of course, never truly free.

The bottle was my idea. I already knew that I needed to do something and I had thought of a letter in a bottle – why not. Then after I saw the film *Message in a Bottle* I decided that was exactly what I would do. The year before, we had spent New Year's Eve on a boat, and I saw these wonderful bottles, and brought one back, I thought it was beautiful. It appealed on a purely aesthetic level; I couldn't put the letter in an ugly bottle. I kept it for over a year. I had realized I needed to do something to let him go, but the whole thing was triggered by a dream, the dream that I mentioned in the letter, I had this beautiful dream about Maurice, and I finally understood that it was time, time to let him go. 'For a long time he travelled between two waters, between two lights . . .' That's because I couldn't let him go, I was holding him back.

So that's when I decided what to do. It took me about two months to write the letter. I've kept the drafts, I read it onto a Dictaphone. In fact when I met with Christine, the message was already all sealed up, so she never saw the letter, she saw only the bottle, with the letter already in it. I gave her the Dictaphone, and I went away while she listened to it. Without Christine at my side I wouldn't have had the strength to carry it through.

The locks of hair I included with the letter – there is one lock from me and one from my son. My hair is the darker lock, his was a little lighter. It's the last lock of hair that I cut from his head when he . . . when he left.

Our family is cursed. The eldest son is always doomed. My grandmother's first son died in an accident aged seventeen, then I lost my son, my niece lost her first son, my cousin lost hers. All were young. Now I have grandchildren, I worry about them.

Maurice was killed in a car accident on 27 August 1981. We had gone on holiday to Spain, we had just come back. Two days after our return the television set had given up the ghost, so my husband and I had decided to buy a new one. Maurice didn't want to come with us so he stayed at home. We went off to buy the set and it took us longer than we expected. Maurice decided to go out on his bike, on the main road, and that's where it happened. When we got back the accident had just occurred. I had my two younger children in the back of the car, aged five and three. When we came back he was lying there on the side of the road, his eyes were open, but he was already in a coma. He never woke up. We went to the hospital. I still didn't understand the gravity of the situation, although I realized that there was a lot of blood. The doctor came out and said, 'Well, it's all over.' Just like that. There was stuff in the corridor, I threw it around, I smashed it all up, I screamed, I went mad, I don't know what I did. We were allowed to see him, but I didn't dare to look, to pull back the covers, to disturb him. I couldn't bear to see. I just looked at his face.

And from that point on I descended into hell.

It never occurred to me that anyone would find my letter in the bottle. It simply never crossed my mind. I thought it would smash in the waves and the fragments of glass and paper would gently disperse through the oceans. I gave it to the sea, to the universe, it was perhaps my way of talking to God. I didn't sign it, I put very few personal details in the letter, not thinking that anyone would ever reply.

That night when my son rang me to tell me that he thought he had just seen my letter, my story, on the television, he asked me what colour bottle I had chosen. I had only told him about it the previous year, though I had written the letter seven years before. We rushed to the Internet to see the programme and there it was; my letter – so intimate, so personal – on the screen. I had put my whole heart, my love, my soul, my innards ("mes tripes") into that letter. It was not only the words that I wrote, for me it was my whole life, my tears, my suffering, all my love and I had cast it forth into the ocean, out into the universe. There was so much of myself in that letter that seeing it on the screen was an enormous shock, a very violent emotion. At the time it was so painful to see it again. I felt violated. I have had to come to terms with the fact that someone was carrying out all these investigations into me, had been looking for me.

We got the book, and there was the letter, in its entirety. I now have three other sons but they were not mentioned. In my draft I had written "the only person in the world (with my other sons) that I was born to love for ever", but when I copied out the letter I somehow left out 'my other sons'. I had to explain to them, apologize.

Now, a few weeks later, I've recovered equilibrium. I've regained my distance, I can smile about it. I can think more calmly, which is why I agreed to meet.

I was always a very attentive mother, very protective. Maurice was eight years older than my next son, so for many years he had been an only child. And the last son was born three years after the accident; he was my saviour. I was nineteen when Maurice was born, and he was my great love. He was my life, I lived through him, we were like accomplices, fused together, we guessed one another's thoughts even without even speaking. It is true I was not very happily married, so all my love was diverted towards my son. He was very gentle, very sweet, a truly lovely boy.

I clung to Maurice, he was my love. It was something so strong when he died, there were only two possibilities for me, death or madness. And I considered both.

For about a year I couldn't even embrace the other two children whom I loved above all else, since I was unable to embrace the other son. I was on a kind of razor blade between the dead and the living, torn between the two.

I underwent psychotherapy for ten years, these were the hardest years, but also the most beautiful, because they permitted me to realize many things, to reconstruct myself. Without that I could not have reached this point.

One is never the same, one's life is smashed. I needed to do a lot of work on myself. What helped to save me was the spiritual journey I have been on throughout these years, a great deal of reading of Hindu and Buddhist texts. I'm not Catholic, though my family was.

And of course I was very angry with Him. There is some kind of superior energy, a cosmic force, and I was furious with Him. Today I am once again happy to be alive, I have my grandchildren and so on. Today I can say, 'I have won.'

I think that this meeting with you today is not chance, there is a deeper reason to all this. It is a beautiful story, and that is the important thing. Perhaps through this book the memory of my son can live once more.

Postscript
Seven Years Later

To my sons . . . to my family . . . to my friends and to all strangers . . .

This is a message, a message of love and hope. May it help to heal, may it smooth the way towards a life of serenity, a life that opens its arms to us if only we dare to look in its direction.

It took me over twenty years to 'deliver' my suffering, more than twenty years during which I lost my footing, skimmed the very brink of madness, visited the depths, plunged into the darkest abyss. I stumbled many a time, picking myself up painfully each time, knees and heart bloodied.

During all these years, I tried as hard as I could to keep on course . . . to steer straight in a stormy sea. My tortured mother's heart didn't know which direction to take. In the depths of darkness my departed son called to me ceaselessly . . . holding out his arms tirelessly, tearing at me with a nameless grief. Meanwhile, on the ship, my other sons clung to the rail in all their despair, never letting go of my hand and praying that I not abandon them. I wore myself out try to be there for them all . . . How much suffering I imposed on all my sons, Maurice included.

A chaotic existence, full of contradictions – what I went through no beast could have survived. During these interminable years, I clung to the rudder, never once setting foot on dry land.

The way has been long . . . very long . . . I drifted far off course, before finally coming to understand the reason for my suffering, understanding that life is offered to us only for one brief moment, that we must live it to the full, whatever it may bring. Living it in half measure would not bring my much-loved son back to life.

This bottle, thrown with all my love, was an acceptance of how things are now, today. For love of Maurice I finally accepted the evidence, I accepted that I must let him go, that he must lie in rest, and be permitted to rise towards the heavens. It was a gesture of conscious love, a gesture of love equally towards my other sons whom I love above all else, a gesture of love also for the life I now lead.

There are still so many things to do, to give, to receive . . .

This bottle was thrown out to sea seven years ago . . . a letter dedicated to my son and to the ocean . . . a letter in which I had put all my love, all my soul, all my grief . . . a very intimate letter which came from the very depths of myself . . .

Never for one instant did I imagine that it would be found . . . and read. But if this message has been able to help parents who have lived through the same tragedy, or has drawn attention to the fragility and preciousness of life, then I am recompensed.

One last thing: these trials help us to move forward, to grow. Life is what we want it to be. Give it a chance.

Acknowledgements

I would like to thank everyone who became involved in this quest. I did not name the people whose advice I sought, because sometimes it was given in confidence, and sometimes I have disagreed with it. Nevertheless I am very grateful for the time and effort spent, and I hope they will not be offended with the conclusions I drew.

Particular thanks to Sioux Peto, for sharing the bottle that she found on the beach, and to Olivier Roussel (www.unebouteillealamer.com) for being such a wise, calm and understanding adviser and intermediary. Above all, thank you to the author of the letter, Maurice's mother, who didn't mean to share her letter in the bottle with anyone, but when she realized that she had, continued to do so with such generosity of spirit.

Sources

Instructions on how to create the best floating bottle are from Ed Sobey, 'Ocean Drogues and Drifters', *Sea Frontiers*, International Oceanographic Foundation, vol. 26, no. 6, November/December 1980.

On the history of letters in bottles, see www.timespub.tc/Astrolabe/Archive/Fall2001/message.htm, especially an article by Nigel Sadler, Director of the Turks & Caicos National Museum, Grand Turk, which has a special collection of messages in bottles.

Wim Kruiswijk's survey ran from 1980 to 1998, and was reported in the *Daily Telegraph*, 21 April 1999.

Queen Elizabeth's official Uncorker of Ocean Bottles is frequently mentioned on the internet but I could find no earlier source than an issue of *Reader's Digest* of the 1970s.

On beachcombing, see Lena Lencek and Gideon Bosker, *The Beach: The History of Paradise on Earth*, London: Secker & Warburg, 1998.

On Livingstone's letter, see Simon Keynes (ed.), *Quentin Keynes: Explorer, film-maker, lecturer and book-collector, 1921–2003*, limited edn, Cambridge, 2004. I am grateful to Professor Keynes for sending me a copy of this beautiful book and for letting me reproduce the letter. See also Christie's auction catalogue, 7 April 2004.

Private Hughes's letter was reported in http://news.bbc.co.uk, 18 May 1999.

Details on the *Lusitania* and on Martin Douglas were from Wilmon Menard, 'Neptune's Sea-Mail Service,' *Sea Frontiers*, International Oceanographic Foundation, vol. 26, no. 6, November/December 1980.

On gospel bombs see Curtis C. Ebbesmeyer's article, 'Leftovers/Evangelical Currents', *Cabinet Magazine*, Issue 4, Autumn 2001, at www.cabinet magazine.org.

The information on *Guinness*® beer bottles was supplied by Diageo GB Press Office.

The quotation 'restlesse mindes are tossed' is from Robert Burton, *The Anatomy of Melancholy*, vol. 1, p. 360, ed. T. C. Faulkner et al., Oxford: Clarendon Press 1989–2000.

The film *Message in a Bottle* is based on the novel by Nicholas Sparks, 1998, screenplay by Gerald Di Pego, directed by Luis Mandoki (Warner Bros). I am grateful to Warner Bros. Entertainment Inc. for permission to quote this from the film.

The quotation on *Waterworld* is taken from Blaise Pascal's *Pensées*, II, 72 (1670), translated by W. F. Trotter at http://eserver.org/philosophy/pascal-pensees.txt. It continues, 'When we think to attach ourselves to any point and to fasten to it, it wavers and leaves us; and if we follow it, it eludes our grasp, slips past us, and vanishes forever. Nothing stays for us. This is our natural condition and yet most contrary to our inclination; we burn with desire to find solid ground and an ultimate sure foundation whereon to build a tower reaching to the Infinite. But our whole groundwork cracks, and the earth opens to abysses.' The link between Pascal and *Waterworld* was made by Patrizia A. Muscogiuri, 'Cinematographic Seas: Metaphors of Crossing and Shipwreck on the Big Screen (1990–2001)', in Bernhard Klein (ed.), *Fictions of the Sea: Critical Perspectives on the Ocean in British Literature and Culture*, Aldershot: Ashgate 2002, pp. 203–20.

The quotations from Gilles Perrault were found on www.adminet.com.

The information on tides is taken from *Macmillan-Reeds Nautical Almanac 2002*, eds. Basil D'Oliveira, Brian Goulder, Edward Lee-Elliott, Imsworth: Nautical Data Ltd, 2001.

There is an article on Curtis Ebbesmeyer in http://news.nationalgeo graphic.com/news/2001/06/0619_seacargo.html. Information on rubber duck travelling speeds came from *The Hawk Eye*, 17 August 2003, at www.thehawk eye.com. Sea bean fanatics congregate at www.seabean.com.

Pelton, *Maurice est mort*, Rodez: Editions Rouergue 2003, is reviewed at http://www.ricochet-jeunes.org.

Simon Leys's *La mer dans la littérature française*, Paris: Plon, 2003, 2 vols, is an invaluable guide to the subject, and several of the extracts quoted were initially sourced from here. The reference to the two infinities is from *Les Misérables* (1862), part I, book 2, VIII. *La mer et le vent* was published in 1865. Jules Michelet's quotation is from Leys, vol. I, p. 540, 'en sortant d'elle' and 'La mer et le c*** de ma femme: mes deux infinis.'

On graphology, see Joe Nickell, *Detecting Forgery: Forensic Investigation of Documents*, Kentucky: University Press, 1996; on its lack of accuracy, see p. 39. The earlier sources mentioned by Nickell are F. E. Inbau, A. A. Moenssens and L. E. Vitullo, *Scientific Police Investigation*, New York: Chilton Book Co., 1972.

On DNA, see Samantha Weinberg, *Pointing from the Grave: A True Story of Murder and DNA*, London: Hamish Hamilton, 2003; P. Gill, P. L. Ivanov, C. Kimpton, R. Piercy, N. Benson, G. Tully, I. Evett, E. Hagelberg, K. Sullivan, 'Identification of the remains of the Romanov family by DNA analysis', *Nature Genetics*, 6(2), February 1994, pp. 130–5.

On the tarot, see Will Adcock, Andy Baggott, Staci Mendoza and David Bourne, *How to Predict the Future*, London: Hermes House, 2003, and on the Sabian symbols and Dane Rudhyar, see www.zodiacal.com.

Tom Davis, 'ESDA and the analysis of contested interview notes', *Forensic Linguistics* 1 (1994), pp. 71–89, contains a detailed description of the working of the ESDA machine and Davis's ground-breaking use of it.

On teleradiesthesia, see www.themystica.com.

The quotation on p. 236 is from Milton's *Paradise Lost*, 2.891–4: 'The secrets of the hoary deep, a dark/Illimitable ocean without bound/Without dimension, where length, breadth, and highth,/And time and place are lost'.

All photographs, unless otherwise credited, are the author's own.